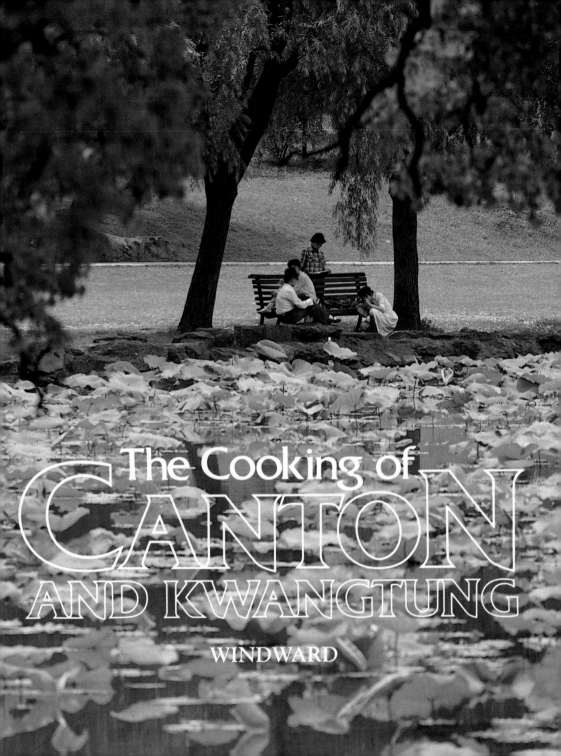

The Cooking of
CANTON
AND KWANGTUNG

WINDWARD

Edited by Carol Jacobson

Windward
an imprint owned by WH Smith & Son Limited
Registered No 237811 England
Trading as WHS Distributors,
St John's House, East Street, Leicester, LE1 6NE.

Printed in Singapore by Tien Mah Litho Printing Co
(Pte) Ltd, 2 Jalan Jentera Jurong Town. Singapore.

Introduction

The southern culinary style of China includes the cooking of Kuangtang (Guangdong) province and surrounding areas, collectively known as Ling-nan in ancient times. The culinary capital of this area and probably of all China is Canton (Gaungzhou) which boasts more restaurants and more original dishes than any other city in China.

The southern region is geographically blessed with optimum conditions for supporting a gourmet cuisine. Rich soil, abundant rainfall and dense vegetation produce a broad range of exotic plants and animals unavailable elsewhere in China. Its location on the coast also gives access to fresh seafoods from the South China Sea.

Among the main ingredients which commonly appear on the southern menu are fish and crustaceans from the ocean and from the ponds and paddies come chicken and ducks. From the vegetable kingdom come an incredible variety of fresh vegetables: the green leafy varieties with crispy textures are especially favoured. Wild game provides yet another source of primary ingredients: civet, racoon, bear, elephant, snake, parrots, monkeys and many other creatures appear in the Cantonese kitchen.

Cantonese chefs are masters of fragrant sauces and spicy dips, a custom which permits each diner to control the flavours himself. Southern cooking places greater emphasis on the colour and overall appearance of dishes than any other region of China and southern flavours are the least contrived relying almost entirely on the fresh-natural flavours of the main ingredients and the skill required to bring them out without resorting to heavy use of condiments.

It is without doubt the most elaborate of Chinese regional cuisines and the most familiar to the Western world. This book gives readers a taste of the rich treasure trove of ingredients which has led logically to the evolution of China's most refined and diverse cuisine.

Contents

Poultry

CRISP SKIN CHICKEN

1 1½ kg (3 lb) plump chicken	**Glaze:**
2 spice bags (five-spice powder)	2½ tablespoons malt sugar (golden syrup,
2 spring onions (scallions), trimmed and cut in halves	clear honey or light corn syrup)
	1½ tablespoons white vinegar
3 thick slices fresh ginger, bruised	1 teaspoon Chinese pepper-salt (page 50)
8 cups (2 litres) deep-frying oil	2 tablespoons boiling water
fresh coriander (optional)	
shredded spring onion (scallion)	

Place chicken breast down in a saucepan with spice bags, spring onions, and ginger. Cover with water, add a pinch of salt and bring to boil. Simmer for 5 minutes, then remove from heat and leave in water to gently poach for 15-20 minutes. Drain and transfer to a colander to cool and dry.

Mix glaze ingredients together, heating slightly if malt sugar is slow to dissolve. Tie a string around neck of chicken and suspend in a breezy place over a drip tray. Pour glaze slowly and evenly over chicken, making sure that some goes into the cavity. Leave to dry for about 5 hours. The skin should feel quite dry and firm.

Heat oil to moderately hot and immerse the chicken completely. Cook for at least 10 minutes, turning once or twice, until skin is a rich red brown and meat is cooked through, but remaining moist and a slightly pink colour. Lift out carefully and drain well. Use cooking chopsticks or the handles of two wooden spoons when moving the chicken as metal utensils may tear the skin.

Cut chicken in halves, then divide into bite-sized pieces, cutting through bones. Or debone completely before cutting into bite-sized pieces. Assemble on serving plate in the shape of a chicken. Garnish with fresh coriander and shredded spring onion and serve with a Chinese pepper-salt dip.

CHICKEN SOUTH CHINA-STYLE

1 1¼ kg (2½ lb) chicken (only the skin is required for this dish)	**Seasoning B:**
	¼ teaspoon salt
625 g (1¼ lb) raw peeled prawns, finely minced (ground)	pinch of m.s.g. (optional)
	½ teaspoon rice wine or dry sherry
75 g (2½ oz) pork fat, finely minced (ground)	¼ cup (2 fl oz) chicken stock
45 g (1½ oz) cooked ham, finely shredded	**Sauce:**
1 tablespoon finely chopped fresh coriander	1 tablespoon rendered chicken fat (chicken grease) (optional)
2 tablespoons frying oil	
280 g (9 oz) fresh spinach leaves	⅓ cup chicken stock
Seasoning A:	¼ teaspoon salt
¾ teaspoon salt	pinch of ground black pepper
½ teaspoon m.s.g. (optional)	½ teaspoon cornflour (cornstarch)
⅓ teaspoon ground black pepper	
1 teaspoon ginger wine	

Skin the chicken, reserving meat for another use. Cut skin into four even-sized pieces. Mix prawn meat and pork fat together and add seasoning A. Mix well and leave for 15 minutes. Spread over chicken skin leaving a wide border all around and garnish with ham and coriander. Roll up and squeeze into sausage shapes, then sew up or secure the ends with toothpicks.

Set rolls in an oiled dish and place on a rack to steam over rapidly boiling water for 20 minutes, then lift out and cut into thick slices.

Sauté spinach in oil for 2 minutes, then add seasoning B and cover. Simmer until tender, then arrange around chicken.

Wipe out wok and add chicken fat, if used, or 1 tablespoon of oil and remaining sauce ingredients, pre-mixed. Bring to boil and simmer until thickened, then pour over chicken rolls and serve.

SALT-BAKED CHICKEN

1 1¼ kg (2½ lb) plump chicken	**Seasoning B:**
2 dried or fresh lotus leaves	⅓ teaspoon salt
3 spring onions (scallions), trimmed and cut in halves	¼ teaspoon m.s.g. (optional)
4 thick slices fresh ginger	½ teaspoon sugar
4 kg (8 lb) rock or coarse salt	1 teaspoon rice wine or dry sherry
155 g (5 oz) fresh broccoli, cut into florets	2 tablespoons chicken stock or water
Seasoning A:	1 teaspoon cornflour (cornstarch)
½ teaspoon m.s.g. (optional)	
½ teaspoon white pepper	
1¼ teaspoons sugar	
1 tablespoon rice wine	
1 tablespoon finely chopped spring onion (scallion)	
½ teaspoon grated fresh ginger	

Rub the skin of chicken with seasoning A. Leave for 1 hour to marinate. Soak dried lotus leaves, if used, in boiling water until softened, or blanch fresh leaves in boiling water for 1 minute and drain well. Stuff the spring onions and ginger into cavity and wrap chicken in the drained leaves. Heat salt in a large saucepan or wok taking care not to let it smoke. Make a cavity in the centre and place chicken in this. Cover with salt, then cover saucepan and cook over moderate heat for 20-25 minutes. Scrape away salt, then turn chicken, re-cover with salt and bake a further 20-25 minutes. Remove chicken and discard leaves.

Cut chicken into bite-sized pieces, cutting through bones. Simmer broccoli in boiling water for 2 minutes. Drain and sauté in a wok with a little oil and seasoning B for a further 2 minutes, then arrange around chicken on a serving plate. Serve at once.

WHOLE CHICKEN STUFFED WITH GLUTINOUS RICE

1 1¼ kg (2½ lb) chicken	**Seasoning:**
125 g (4 oz) glutinous rice, soaked for 1 hour	¾ teaspoon salt
4 dried black mushrooms, soaked for 25 minutes	½ teaspoon m. s. g. (optional)
2 tablespoons rendered chicken fat (chicken grease), or lard	½ teaspoon sugar
	1 tablespoon light soy sauce
3 spring onions (scallions), trimmed and diced	½ teaspoon rice wine or dry sherry
3 slices fresh ginger, chopped	
45 g (1½ oz) Chinese or cured (Smithfield) ham, diced	
1 tablespoon dark soy sauce	
cornflour (cornstarch)	
8 cups (2 litres) deep-frying oil	

Clean and debone the chicken. Rinse out with boiling water and turn inside out. Trim off some of the thicker parts of meat and cut into small dice. Place rice, with water to cover, in a dish and set on a rack in a steamer until almost cooked through, about 35 minutes. Squeeze water from mushrooms and remove stems, dice the caps.

Heat chicken fat in a wok and stir-fry onion and ginger for 1 minute. Add diced chicken and stir-fry until it changes colour, then add mushrooms and ham and fry for 1 minute. Mix in seasoning ingredients and rice and stir-fry for a further 1 minute. Remove to a plate to cool.

Stuff rice mixture into chicken and sew up opening or secure with poultry pins. Rub with dark soy sauce and place in a deep dish. Set on a rack and steam over high heat for about 50 minutes. Remove, wipe skin and coat lightly with cornflour.

Heat oil to smoking point and quickly deep-fry the chicken, completely immersed if possible, until crisp and golden brown. Remove and drain. Place breast up and slash across breast in two places to expose filling.

SLICED CHICKEN WITH CHRYSANTHEMUM PETALS

280 g (9 oz) boneless chicken breast

30 g (1 oz) white chrysanthemum petals

4 cups (1 litre) deep-frying oil

1 tablespoon softened lard

1 spring onion (scallion), trimmed and shredded

1 slice fresh ginger, shredded

¾ teaspoon rice wine or dry sherry

Seasoning A:

1 egg white, beaten

½ teaspoon salt

½ teaspoon m.s.g. (optional)

pinch of white pepper

½ teaspoon rice wine or dry sherry

½ teaspoon cornflour (cornstarch)

Seasoning B/Sauce:

¼ cup (2 fl oz) chicken stock

½ teaspoon salt

¼ teaspoon m.s.g. (optional)

¾ teaspoon sugar

½ teaspoon cornflour (cornstarch)

Slice the chicken across the grain fairly thinly and place in a dish with seasoning A. Mix well and leave to marinate for 15 minutes.

Wash chrysanthemum petals and dry.

Heat oil to moderately hot and deep-fry chicken until it turns white, about 45 seconds. Remove and pour off oil. Add lard to pan and stir-fry spring onion and ginger briefly. Sizzle wine onto sides of pan and return the chicken. Stir-fry for 1 minute, then add pre-mixed seasoning B/sauce and bring to the boil, stirring. Add petals and stir for a few seconds, then serve.

DICED CHICKEN AND CASHEW NUTS

250 g (8 oz) boneless chicken

2 cups (16 fl oz) frying oil

45 g (1½ oz) raw cashew nuts or peanuts

12 snow peas

12 canned champignons, drained

4 canned water chestnuts, drained

45 g (1½ oz) canned bamboo shoots, drained and sliced

280 g (9 oz) young bok choy or choy sum

Seasoning A:

½ teaspoon salt

¼ teaspoon m.s.g. (optional)

¾ teaspoon sugar

1 teaspoon light soy sauce

1 teaspoon rice wine or dry sherry

½ teaspoon cornflour (cornstarch)

Seasoning B/Sauce:

¼ cup (2 fl oz) chicken stock or water

½ teaspoon dark soy sauce

½ teaspoon salt

¼ teaspoon m.s.g. (optional)

¼ teaspoon sugar

pinch of ground black pepper

½ teaspoon cornflour (cornstarch)

Cut chicken into small cubes, mix with seasoning A and leave for 20 minutes. Heat oil to fairly hot and deep-fry the nuts for about 2 minutes, until light gold in colour. Remove and drain well. Leave to cool. String the snow peas. Cut champignons in halves horizontally, cut water chestnuts into three pieces each, horizontally. Rinse vegetables well and cut stems into 5 cm (2 in) lengths.

Heat a wok and add 2 tablespoons of oil. When smoking hot add chicken and stir-fry for 2 minutes. Remove from pan and add the *bok choy*. Splash in a little water, cover pan and cook on fairly high heat, shaking pan to keep the vegetables turning, for 1½-2 minutes. Add remaining vegetables and stir-fry for 30-45 seconds. Add pre-mixed seasoning B/sauce and simmer briefly, then return chicken and continue to cook until sauce thickens. Stir in cashews and serve.

QUICK-FRIED CHICKEN SHREDS WITH ONION

375 g (12 oz) boneless chicken breast	**Seasoning B/Sauce:**
1 large brown onion	¼ cup (2 fl oz) chicken stock
¼ cup (2 fl oz) frying oil	2 tablespoons tomato sauce (ketchup) or 1 tablespoon light soy sauce
Seasoning A:	½-¾ teaspoon chilli oil
1 egg white	¾ teaspoon sesame oil
½ teaspoon salt	1 teaspoon cornflour (cornstarch)
¼ teaspoon m.s.g. (optional)	
pinch of white pepper	
1 teaspoon rice wine or dry sherry	
½ teaspoon cornflour (cornstarch)	

Slice chicken, then cut into narrow shreds. Mix with seasoning A and leave to marinate for 15 minutes.

Peel onion and cut in halves from stem to root. Trim away root section and cut into thin slices, then separate the layers.

Heat oil in a wok and fry chicken on moderately high heat until white, about 1¼ minutes. Remove and keep warm. Add onion to pan and stir-fry for 1½ minutes on high heat, then pour in pre-mixed seasoning B/sauce and bring to boil. Return chicken and stir on high heat until sauce thickens.

Serve at once.

SWEET AND SOUR SAUCE

1 tablespoon frying oil	⅓ cup sugar
1 tablespoon finely chopped Chinese pickles	⅓ cup white vinegar
1 tablespoon finely chopped fresh ginger	¼ teaspoon salt
½ teaspoon crushed garlic (optional)	1 tablespoon liquid from Chinese pickles
½ cup (4 fl oz) chicken stock	2½ teaspoons cornflour (cornstarch)

Mix all ingredients in a saucepan and bring to the boil. Simmer for about 3 minutes.

STEAMED CHICKEN DRESSED WITH SPRING ONIONS AND GINGER

1¼ kg (2½ lb) chicken	**Seasoning:**
5 spring onions (scallions), trimmed and shredded	2 teaspoons salt
	1 teaspoon m. s. g. (optional)
6 slices fresh ginger, shredded	½ teaspoon sugar
¼ cup (2 fl oz) frying oil	1 tablespoon rice wine or dry sherry
	2 tablespoons finely chopped spring onion (scallion)
	1 tablespoon grated fresh ginger

Rub chicken all over with pre-mixed seasoning. Leave to marinate for 1 hour, then place breast up in a dish and set on a rack to steam over rapidly boiling water for 45-50 minutes, then drain and remove to a cutting board. Cut into bite-sized pieces and assemble on a serving plate in the shape of a chicken.

Garnish with shredded spring onion and ginger. Heat oil to smoking point and pour over chicken. Serve at once.

SWEET CORN AND CHICKEN SOUP

1 500 g (1 lb) can sweet corn kernels	**Seasoning:**
90 g (3 oz) coarsely minced chicken breast	1½ teaspoons salt
4 cups (1 litre) chicken stock	¾ teaspoon m. s. g. (optional)
¼ cup cornflour (cornstarch)	1 tablespoon light soy sauce

Drain corn and crush lightly in a mortar or food processor. Pour into a saucepan and add chicken, stock, seasonings. Bring to the boil and simmer for 3 minutes, then add cornflour mixed with an equal quantity of cold water and simmer until soup thickens and turns clear. Pour into a soup tureen and serve.

SPICED SALT

4 tablespoons table salt	1½-2 teaspoons five spice powder

Dry — fry salt in a wok over low to moderate heat until well warmed. Stir constantly to avoid burning. Remove from heat and stir in five spice powder. Cool, then store in an airtight jar.

HONEY-BASTED ROAST DUCK

1 1½ kg (3 lb) duck	**Sauce:**
⅓ cup clear honey	⅓ cup chicken stock
1½ tablespoons boiling water	¼ cup (2 fl oz) light soy sauce
Seasoning:	1½ teaspoons rice wine or dry sherry
3 cubes fermented beancurd with the liquid, mashed	⅓ teaspoon salt
	⅓ teaspoon m.s.g. (optional)
1 teaspoon salt	1 teaspoon sugar
½ teaspoon m.s.g. (optional)	1½ teaspoons cornflour (cornstarch)
1 tablespoon sugar	
¼ teaspoon ground black pepper	

Make a fairly large opening near the rear of the duck and work through this to rub the pre-mixed seasoning thoroughly over insides. Leave for 2 hours.

Tie a string around duck's neck and suspend above a drip tray. Pour boiling water over skin, taking care not to allow any inside, as it will wash away the seasonings. When skin has dried slightly, pour on pre-mixed honey and boiling water, working slowly and thoroughly over the entire outside of the duck and allowing a little to run inside. Hang duck in a well-ventilated place until the skin is dry.

Fix the duck onto a rotisserie bar set over a charcoal fire (or cook on rotisserie in a preheated oven 200°C (400°F/Gas 6) for 25 minutes, then reduce to low, 120°C (250°F/Gas ½) and roast for a further 55 minutes. Cook, turning constantly, until duck is just cooked and skin crisp and a deep golden colour. Remove to a cutting board and cut in halves, then slice through the bones into bite-sized pieces and arrange on a plate.

Bring sauce ingredients to the boil and simmer until thickened. Pour over duck just before serving. Serve with additional condiments of hot mustard and plum sauce.

HOME STYLE SIMMER-STEWED DUCK

1 1¾ kg (3½ lb) duck	**Seasoning A:**
500 g (1 lb) fatty pork or 'five flowered' belly pork (fresh bacon)	¼ cup (2 fl oz) light soy sauce
	2 tablespoons rice wine or dry sherry
8 cups (2 litres) deep-frying oil	**Seasoning B:**
30 g (1 oz) Chinese red dates, or use black dates or Japanese salted plums (umeboshi)	3 cups (24 fl oz) chicken stock
	1 tablespoon sugar
45 g (1½ oz) salted mustard root, washed and diced	¾ teaspoon m.s.g. (optional)
2 spring onions (scallions), trimmed and sliced	½ teaspoon ground black pepper
5 slices fresh ginger	¼ cup soybean paste
6 young bok choy or lettuce	
cornflour (cornstarch)	

Blanch duck in boiling water for 2 minutes. Drain and rub with some of the seasoning A ingredients, reserving that which is not used. Blanch the pork and drain well. Wipe dry and also rub with seasoning A ingredients. Mix any remaining seasoning A with the seasoning B ingredients, except the soybean paste, and set aside.

Heat oil to fairly hot. Deep-fry duck and pork separately until well coloured. Drain well. Cut pork into cubes and stuff into cavity of duck, then place duck, breast down, in a casserole.

Transfer 2 tablespoons of oil to another pan and sauté the soybean paste for 1 minute. Add seasoning B ingredients and bring to the boil. Pour over duck. Add dates, mustard root, spring onions and ginger and add water to just cover. Bring to boil and simmer, tightly covered, until duck is completely tender, about 2 hours. Lift out duck, cut open and remove the pork. Reserve the stock. Shred duck meat by hand, discarding the bones. Pile duck in the centre of a dish and surround with pork. Set on a rack and steam over gently boiling water for 15 minutes. In the meantime, strain the reserved stock into a wok and reduce to about ¾ cup.

In another pan, sauté vegetables in 2 tablespoons of oil, adding a pinch of salt and sugar and a dash of rice wine or dry sherry. Arrange on top of meat and steam a further 5 minutes. Thicken sauce with a thin solution of cornflour and cold water and pour over dish.

CHOPPED DUCK WITH LOTUS ROOT AND VEGETABLES

1 1¾ kg (3½ lb) duck	**Seasoning B:**
90 g (3 oz) canned lotus root, drained	¼ cup (2 fl oz) chicken stock
45 g (1½ oz) Chinese or cured (Smithfield) ham (optional)	½ teaspoon salt
	2 tablespoons light soy sauce
90 g (3 oz) squash or winter melon	1 teaspoon rice wine or dry sherry
60 g (2 oz) canned champignons, drained*	2 spring onions (scallions), trimmed and sliced
2 tablespoons softened lard or frying oil	2 slices fresh ginger
Seasoning A:	
1 egg white, beaten	
¼ teaspoon salt	
¼ teaspoon m.s.g. (optional)	
1 tablespoon cold water	
1 tablesploon cornflour (cornstarch)	

Debone duck and cut into 4 cm (1⅔ in) squares. Place in a dish with seasoning A and leave for 20 minutes to marinate.

Slice lotus roots lengthwise and cut into 4 cm (1⅔ in) squares. Cut ham into the same sized pieces, if used. Peel and cube the squash. Slice champignons in halves horizontally, or squeeze water from soaked mushrooms, remove stems and cut caps into quarters.

Arrange duck, mushrooms, and ham, if used, in a large bowl and add seasoning B. Cover and set on a rack to steam over rapidly boiling water for 35 minutes, discard onion and ginger.

Blanch lotus root in boiling water and drain well. Heat lard in a wok and stir-fry lotus root for 1 minute. Add drained duck, mushrooms, and ham, reserving stock, and stir-fry together for 2 minutes. Add melon and stir-fry for a further 2 minutes, then pour in reserved stock and reduce heat. Simmer together until melon is tender, then thicken sauce with a thin solution of cornflour and cold water. Check seasonings and serve.

* Or use 6-8 dried black mushrooms, soaked for 25 minutes.

DUCK LIVERS WITH
HOT PEPPER SAUCE

315 g (10 oz) fresh duck livers	**Seasoning B/Sauce:**
4 cups (1 litre) deep-frying oil	1/2 cup (4 fl oz) chicken stock
1 tablespoon sesame oil	2 tablespoons light soy sauce
3 spring onions (scallions), trimmed and diced	1 1/2 teaspoons dark soy sauce
2 slices fresh ginger, chopped	1 teaspoon chilli oil (or less, to taste)
1/2 teaspoon ground black pepper (optional)	1/2 teaspoon salt
1/2 teaspoon crushed garlic	1/4 teaspoon ground black pepper
Seasoning A:	3/4 teaspoon sugar
1/3 teaspoon salt	1 teaspoon cornflour (cornstarch)
1/4 teaspoon m.s.g. (optional)	
1/4 teaspoon ground black pepper	
1 tablespoon rice wine or dry sherry	

Blanch livers in boiling water, drain and cut into bite-sized pieces. Place in a dish with seasoning A and leave for 30 minutes.

Deep-fry livers in smoking hot deep oil for 30-45 seconds. Drain and pour off all but 2 1/2 tablespoons of oil. Add sesame oil and sauté onions, ginger, and garlic for 1 minute. Add livers and sauté briefly, then pour in pre-mixed seasoning B/sauce and bring to the boil.

Reduce heat and simmer for about 5 minutes until livers are tender and sauce well reduced. Stir in black pepper, if used, and serve.

CANTONESE ROAST DUCK

1 1½ kg (3 lb) duck	**Glaze:**
Seasoning:	2½ tablespoons malt sugar
2 tablespoons soybean paste	¼ cup (2 fl oz) white vinegar
1 tablespoon rice wine or dry sherry	1½ tablespoons boiling water
1 teaspoon salt	
1 teaspoon m.s.g. (optional)	
1 tablespoon sugar	
½ teaspoon powdered licorice root, or 1 small piece licorice root (optional), or use 1 star anise	
3 tablespoons finely chopped spring onion	
1 tablespoon finely chopped fresh ginger	
1¼ teaspoons crushed garlic	

Blanch duck in boiling water for 2 minutes. Remove and drain well. Tie a string around its neck, passing it beneath the wings to hold them away from the body. Hang in a well-ventilated place over a drip tray.

Mix seasoning and smear thickly over the inside of duck. Secure the lower opening with poultry pins, or sew up.

Mix glaze, stirring over a pan of boiling water if malt sugar is slow to dissolve. Slowly pour over duck's skin to coat evenly. Catch the drips and brush these onto skin until thickly coated. Leave to dry for 1 hour.

Place duck, breast down, on a rack in a baking tin and bake in a preheated hot oven at 200°C (400°F/Gas 6) for 20 minutes, then reduce the heat to 170°C (325°F/Gas 3) and roast a further 55 minutes, turning the duck once. If preferred, secure the duck on rotisserie pin and cook on high heat for 25 minutes, then reduce to low for remainder of cooking.

Drain pan juices into a wok and bring to the boil. Supplement with a little chicken stock or water if the amount is small. Check seasonings and keep hot.

Cut duck into serving portions or bite-sized pieces, as preferred, and arrange on a serving plate. Pour on sauce and serve at once.

DUCK SIMMERED IN YELLOW RICE WINE

¼ cup (2 fl oz) light soy sauce	**Seasoning:**
⅔ cup yellow rice wine (Shao Hsing)	2 tablespoons light soy sauce
1 1½ kg (3 lb) duck	2 spring onions (scallions), trimmed and sliced
6 cups (1½ litres) deep-frying oil	3 thick slices fresh ginger, bruised
7 cups (1¾ litres) chicken stock or water	1½ teaspoons salt
cornflour (cornstarch)	2 teaspoons sugar
	¾ teaspoon m.s.g. (optional)

Pour the soy sauce and wine over duck, rubbing inside and out and leave for 1 hour, then drain liquid into a dish and add the remaining seasoning ingredients.

Heat oil to smoking point and deep-fry duck until well coloured red. Lift out and drain well. Place duck, breast downwards, on a bamboo rack in a casserole and add the stock and seasoning ingredients. Bring to the boil, then cook on low heat for at least 1½ hours until duck is completely tender.

Carefully lift out and cut into serving portions. Reduce sauce to about 1 cup. Check seasonings and thicken with a paste of cornflour and cold water. Pour over duck and serve.

Diced Chicken and Cashew Nuts (recipe page 11)
and Watercress and Liver Soup (recipe page 63)

Seafood

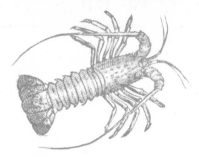

LOBSTER WITH BLACK BEANS AND CHILLIES

1 750 g (1½ lb) fresh lobster	**Seasoning/Sauce:**
1 tablespoon fermented black beans	¼ cup (2 fl oz) chicken stock
¾ teaspoon crushed garlic	1 teaspoon ginger wine
1 teaspoon sugar	¼ teaspoon salt
¼ cup(2 fl oz) frying oil	¼ teaspoon ground black pepper
1 spring onion (scallion), trimmed and diced	¾ teaspoon cornflour (cornstarch)
1-2 fresh red chilli peppers, thinly sliced	
4 slices fresh ginger, shredded	
¾ teaspoon rice wine or dry sherry	
1 tablespoon light soy sauce	

Cut lobster in halves and discard inedible parts. Scoop out flesh and cut into cubes. Scrape out shell and drop it, with the head, into a saucepan of boiling water. Cook until bright red, then drain, rinse with cold water and brush again to remove any residue. Rinse in cold, salted water and dry. Place on a serving plate.

Chop black beans finely. Mix with garlic and sugar and fry in a wok with oil for 1 minute. Add lobster pieces and stir-fry until white and firm, about 2 minutes, then remove. Reheat wok and stir-fry spring onion, chilli pepper and ginger together for 1 minute, sizzle wine and soy sauce onto sides of wok and stir in, then add pre-mixed seasoning/sauce and bring to the boil. Return lobster and black beans and simmer until sauce is thickened.

Spoon into the lobster shell and serve at once.

SLICED FISH SAUTÉED WITH BLACK BEANS

315 g (10 oz) boneless white fish fillets	**Seasoning B/Sauce:**
1 large white onion	¼ cup (2 fl oz) chicken stock
1 large green capsicum (bell pepper)	2 tablespoons light soy sauce
1 tablespoon fermented black beans	⅓ teaspoon salt
1 teaspoon finely chopped garlic	1½ teaspoons sugar
3 cups (24 fl oz) deep-frying oil	½ teaspoon m.s.g. (optional)
1 slice fresh ginger, finely shredded	
2 teaspoons rice wine or dry sherry	
Seasoning A:	
1 egg white, beaten	
½ teaspoon salt	
½ teaspoon m.s.g. (optional)	
pinch of white pepper	
1 tablespoon cornflour (cornstarch)	
2 tablespoons vegetable oil	

Slice fish, cutting across fillets at a sharp angle to produce slices of about 7.5 x 2.5 cm (3 x 1 in) and about 1 cm (⅓ in) thick. Place in a dish and add seasoning A, mix well and leave for 15 minutes to marinate.

Peel onion and trim away root section, then cut into slices from stem to root and separate the pieces. Cut pepper in halves, remove stem and seed core and trim away inner white ribs. Shred finely. Wash black beans, dry on kitchen paper and chop lightly. Mix with garlic.

Heat oil to fairly hot and fry fish in a basket for 45 seconds to 1 minute, until crisped on the surface and just cooked through. Drain and set aside. Pour off all but 3 tablespoons of oil and sautée onion and ginger for 1 minute, then add black bean mixture and sautée for 30 seconds. Sizzle wine onto sides of pan and stir in.

Add shredded pepper and sauté until just softened. Pour in the pre-mixed seasoning B/ sauce and bring to the boil. Return fish slices and heat thoroughly. Serve.

SAUTÉED FIVE SHREDS
WITH SLICED FISH

185 g (6 oz) boneless white fish	**Seasoning A:**
1 medium carrot	1 egg white, beaten
1 medium green capsicum (bell pepper)	½ teaspoon salt
3 dried black mushrooms, soaked for 25 minutes	½ teaspoon m. s. g. (optional)
30 g (1 oz) fresh bean sprouts	¼ teaspoon white pepper
1 large white onion	1½ teaspoons rice wine or dry sherry
3 cups (24 fl oz) deep-frying oil	1 tablespoon cornflour (cornstarch)
2 tablespoons sesame oil	**Seasoning B/Sauce:**
1½ teaspoons rice wine or dry sherry	⅓ cup chicken stock
	1 teaspoon sesame oil (optional)
	½ teaspoon salt
	½ teaspoon m. s. g. (optional)
	¼ teaspoon ground black pepper
	¾ teaspoon cornflour (cornstarch)

Cut fish into narrow strips, then into pieces about 5 cm (2 in) long. Place in a dish with seasoning A, mix well and leave for 15 minutes.

Peel the carrot. Remove seed core, stem, and inner white ribs of the pepper, squeeze water from mushrooms and remove stems. Shred the three vegetables. Remove roots and pods from bean sprouts, if preferred. Cut onion in halves from stem to root. Trim away root section, then cut into thin slices and separate the pieces.

Heat oil to moderately hot and add the sesame oil. Fry fish until it turns white, about 45 seconds. Drain well. Pour off all but 3 tablespoons of oil and fry shredded vegetables on moderate heat for 3 minutes, stirring continually. Add fish and sizzle wine onto sides of pan.

Pour in pre-mixed seasoning B/sauce and stir until sauce thickens.

SHRIMP SAUSAGE SAUTÉED WITH BEAN SPROUTS

185 g (6 oz) raw peeled shrimps	**Seasoning B/Sauce:**
¼ cup (2 fl oz) softened lard or frying oil	⅓ cup chicken stock
2 spring onions (scallions), trimmed and shredded	1 teaspoon rice wine or dry sherry
	1 teaspoon sesame oil
4 slices fresh ginger, shredded	⅓ teaspoon salt
185 g (6 oz) fresh bean sprouts	¼ teaspoon m.s.g. (optional)
Seasoning A:	¼ teaspoon white pepper
1 egg white, beaten	¼ teaspoon sugar
¼ teaspoon salt	1 teaspoon cornflour (cornstarch)
½ teaspoon m.s.g. (optional)	
pinch of white pepper	
1 tablespoon cornflour (cornstarch)	
1 tablespoon rendered chicken fat (chicken grease), or use lard	

Chop the shrimp in a food processor or by using 2 cleavers. Add seasoning A and mix thoroughly until mixture is smooth. Heat a saucepan of lightly salted water to boiling, then reduce the heat until gently simmering.

Transfer the shrimp paste to a piping bag fitted with a large plain nozzle and pipe a continuous stream of paste in a circle into simmering water. Cook for 1 minute, then lift out and rinse in cold water. Leave to cool, then cut into pieces about 5 cm (2 in) long.

Heat wok and add lard. Sauté spring onions and ginger for 45 seconds, then push to one side of pan and add bean sprouts and sauté until softened. Remove. Reheat pan and sauté shrimp sausage for 1½ minutes, until lightly coloured. Add pre-mixed seasoning B/sauce and return spring onions, ginger, and bean sprouts and mix well. Simmer until sauce has thickened, then transfer to a warmed serving plate.

SHRIMPS COOKED IN THEIR SHELLS

	Seasoning:
375 g (12 oz) raw shrimps, in their shells	
5 cups (1 1/4 litres) deep-frying oil	1 1/4 teaspoons salt
2 spring onions (scallions), shredded	1/2 teaspoon m.s.g. (optional)
3 slices fresh ginger, shredded	1 1/4 teaspoons sugar
1 fresh red chilli pepper, seeds removed and shredded (optional)	1 teaspoon sesame oil (optional)
	1/4 cup (2 fl oz) chicken stock

Remove legs and undershells of shrimps, but leave heads, tails, and top of shells intact. Heat oil to smoking point and fry shrimps in a basket for 25 seconds. Remove and drain.

Pour off all but 2 tablespoons of oil. Reduce heat to moderate and fry spring onions, ginger, and chilli, if used, for 1 minute, stirring frequently. Add shrimps and fry for 30 seconds, then add seasoning ingredients and simmer until liquid has almost evaporated.

STEAMED FRESH PRAWNS

	Sauce Dip:
750 g (1 1/2 lb) large green prawns (shrimps) in the shell	
	1/3 cup dark soy sauce
1 tablespoon frying oil	2 1/2 tablespoons vegetable oil
	1 teaspoon sugar
	2 fresh red chilli peppers

Prepare the sauce first. Thinly slice chillies, discarding seeds. Mix soy sauce, oil, and sugar until amalgamated, then add chillies and pour into several dishes. Set aside. If preferred, chopped spring onion and/or fresh ginger can be used in place of chilli peppers.

Wash prawns in cold, lightly salted water and place in a large dish so that none overlaps. Sprinkle on oil and set dish on a rack in a steamer. Cover and steam over rapidly boiling water for about 8 minutes. The actual cooking time will depend on the size of prawns. Test by opening one after 6 minutes.

Serve prawns straight from steamer with sauce dips and damp napkins or finger bowls.

PRAWNS CLEAR AS CRYSTAL

625 g (1 ¼ lb) green prawns (shrimps) in the shell

1 tablespoon bicarbonate of soda

1 teaspoon salt

1 tablespoon cornflour (cornstarch)

6 spring onions (scallions), trimmed
and finely shredded

5 cm (2 in) piece fresh ginger, finely shredded

small bunch of fresh coriander

oyster sauce*

Chinese shrimp sauce

3 cups (24 fl oz) deep-frying oil

Seasoning/Sauce:

¼ cup (2 fl oz) chicken stock

2 teaspoons rice wine or dry sherry

½ teaspoon sesame oil (optional)

¼ teaspoon salt

½ teaspoon m. s. g. (optional)

pinch of white pepper

Shell prawns and cut in halves lengthwise. Remove veins and place in a dish with water to cover. Add bicarbonate of soda, mix in and leave for 2-3 hours, then rinse well in cold water, gently rubbing on salt and cornflour in the process. Drain and wipe dry with kitchen paper. This process whitens the prawns and eliminates the slight fishy odour.

Arrange shredded onions and ginger on a serving plate. Wash coriander thoroughly, remove stems and set aside for garnish. Make up several dip dishes of oyster sauce and shrimp paste. If shrimp paste is unobtainable, use anchovy sauce or essence.

Bring a saucepan of water to the boil and in another pan heat oil to fairly hot. Place prawns in a wire strainer and dip into boiling water for 30 seconds. Lift out and drain well. Shake in a kitchen towel to absorb excess water, then transfer to a frying basket and dip into hot oil for 10 seconds. Lift out and shake off oil, then return to hot oil for a further 10 seconds. Remove and drain well.

Pour off water and wipe out pan. Add pre-mixed seasoning/sauce and bring to the boil. Simmer briefly, then add prawns and turn quickly in the sauce until glazed. Arrange on the onions and ginger and garnish with fresh coriander. Serve at once with prepared dips.

*Some of the less expensive commercial brands of oyster sauce are not suitable for use as a dipping sauce. The better brands have the strong salty taste necessary when serving straight from the bottle.

STUFFED PRAWNS IN HOT SAUCE

500 g (1 lb) large green prawns (shrimps), in the shell	**Sauce:**
1 teaspoon salt	*¼ cup (2 fl oz) chicken stock*
60 g (2 oz) fatty pork, finely minced (ground)	*2 tablespoons light soy sauce*
2 teaspoons finely chopped cooked ham	*1 teaspoon rice wine or dry sherry*
2 teaspoons finely chopped softened dried mushrooms or champignons	*½-¾ teaspoon chilli oil**
1 large egg, beaten	*¼ teaspoon salt*
cornflour (cornstarch)	*½ teaspoon m.s.g. (optional)*
4 cups (1 litre) deep-frying oil	*½ teaspoon sugar*
	pinch of white pepper
	1 teaspoon cornflour (cornstarch)

Remove heads from prawns and sprinkle them with salt. Set aside. Cut off about 2.5 cm (1 in) of meat from top end of each prawn, de-vein and chop finely. Mix with minced pork and add a dash of salt, m.s.g., if used, and white pepper.

Cut remaining parts of prawns open along back, cutting deep enough so they can be pressed out flat. De-vein and coat lightly with cornflour. Press a portion of prawn and pork mixture onto each, forming into a fanned shape. Garnish with chopped ham and mushrooms and brush with beaten egg. Coat lightly with cornflour.

Heat oil to fairly hot and fry stuffed prawns for 1½ minutes, until golden. Drain and set aside, keeping warm. Pour off all but 2 tablespoons of oil and stir-fry prawn heads for about 3 minutes until bright red and cooked through.

Line up heads on a serving dish and arrange tails near them. Wipe out pan and add 1 table-spoon of oil. Pour in pre-mixed sauce and bring to the boil. Stir until thickened, then pour over prawn tails and serve at once.

* Or substitute 1½ tablespoons hot black bean sauce for the chilli oil and use only 1½-2 tea-spoons of soy sauce.

BRAISED PRAWNS IN GRAVY

500 g (1 lb) green prawns (shrimps), in the shell	**Seasoning B/Sauce:**
1 cup (8 fl oz) frying oil	1 cup (8 fl oz) chicken stock
4 spring onions (scallions), trimmed and sliced	2 tablespoons light soy sauce
4 slices fresh ginger	3/4 teaspoon chilli oil*
Seasoning A:	1 1/2 teaspoons sesame oil
1/3 teaspoon salt	1/4 teaspoon salt
1/4 teaspoon m.s.g. (optional)	3/4 teaspoon sugar
1/4 teaspoon white pepper	1/4 teaspoon white pepper
2 teaspoons sesame oil	1 1/2 teaspoons cornflour (cornstarch)

Peel prawns, leaving heads and tails intact. De-vein with a toothpick, add seasoning A and leave for 15 minutes to marinate.

Heat oil to fairly hot and stir-fry prawns until heads turn bright red, about 1 minute. Remove. Add onions and ginger and stir-fry for 30 seconds, then pour in pre-mixed seasoning B/sauce and bring to the boil. Return the prawns.

Reduce heat and simmer until prawns are tender and sauce thickened. Transfer to a warmed serving dish.

* Or omit the chilli oil and use oyster sauce or hot black bean sauce. Add slightly less soy sauce, to taste.

CRYSTAL PRAWNS

24 medium raw prawns	4 spring onions (scallions)
1 tablespoon ginger wine	2.5 cm (1 in) piece fresh ginger, sliced
1 tablespoon water	1 carrot, sliced
1/4 teaspoon white pepper	oil

Peel prawns leaving heads and tails intact. Cut a deep slit down the back of each prawn and devein. Marinate in ginger wine, water and pepper for 5 minutes. Cut spring onions into 8 cm (3 in) pieces. Shred both ends of each piece and drop into iced water to curl. Cut decorative shapes from carrot and ginger slices. Heat 3 tablespoons oil in a wok and stir fry prawns until they turn pink and curl. Cook until just firm. Do not overcook. Decorate with vegetables and serve with dark soy sauce.

CRABMEAT OMELETTE

	Sauce:
3 egg whites	2 tablespoons chicken stock
2 whole eggs	1 tablespoon oyster sauce
2 tablespoons chicken stock	1/2 teaspoon rice wine or dry sherry
1/4 teaspoon salt	1/2 teaspoon m.s.g. (optional)
2 tablespoons softened lard	1/2 teaspoon sugar, or to taste
1 large spring onion (scallion), trimmed and shredded	pinch of ground black pepper
1 slice fresh ginger, shredded	2/3 teaspoon cornflour (cornstarch)
60 g (2 oz) fresh crabmeat	
15 g (1 oz) crab roe	
1 teaspoon rice wine or dry sherry	

Beat egg whites and whole eggs together and add chicken stock and salt.

Heat half the lard in a wok and sauté spring onion and ginger briefly. Add crabmeat and cook until lightly coloured, then add roe and sizzle wine onto sides of pan and stir in. Remove and keep warm.

Reheat wok and add remaining lard. Pour in egg mixture and cook on moderate heat until lightly coloured underneath, then spread cooked crab over the egg and carefully turn the omelette. Cook the underside until just firm, lift onto a serving plate. It may be cut into quarters to make turning easier.

Wipe out wok and add pre-mixed sauce. Simmer, stirring until thickened, about 45 seconds. Pour over the omelette and serve at once.

STIR-FRIED CRAB FU YUNG

	Seasoning/Sauce:
2 375 g (12 oz) crab	
1 tablespoon ginger wine	¼ cup (2 fl oz) chicken stock
5 cups (1¼ litres) deep-frying oil	1 teaspoon salt
1 spring onion (scallion), trimmed and diced	¼ teaspoon m.s.g. (optional)
3 slices fresh ginger, shredded	¼ teaspoon ground black pepper
2 teaspoons rice wine or dry sherry	½ teaspoon sesame oil (optional)
4 eggs, well beaten	1 teaspoon cornflour (cornstarch)

Wash crabs well and break open. Remove all inedible parts, then chop the crabs through the shells into large pieces. Place in a dish and sprinkle on ginger wine. Leave for 20 minutes.

Heat oil to smoking point and deep-fry crab pieces for 1 minute. Remove and drain well. If preferred, the crab can be stir-fried in ⅓ cup frying oil for 2½ minutes.

Pour off all but 2½ tablespoons of oil and stir-fry spring onion and ginger for 30 seconds, then return crab and add pre-mixed seasoning/sauce and rice wine. Simmer for 2 minutes, then pour in well-beaten eggs and cook without stirring until the eggs are set. Stir lightly and transfer to a serving plate.

STEAMED CRABS WITH GINGER SAUCE

	Ginger Sauce:
6 small crabs	
2 teaspoons rice wine or dry sherry	5 cm (2 in) piece fresh ginger, peeled and minced
2 spring onions (scallions), trimmed and shredded	½ cup (4 fl oz) white vinegar
	1 tablespoon sugar
6 slices fresh ginger, shredded	2 teaspoons sesame oil

Prepare sauce first to allow time for flavours to blend. Mix the four ingredients together, stirring until sugar is completely dissolved. Pour into several small dishes and set aside.

Wash crabs, cut open underneath and remove inedible parts, then crack the claws. Reassemble crabs and place in a large dish. Sprinkle on wine and scatter shredded onion and ginger over the crabs. Set on a rack and steam over high heat for 15 minutes.

Serve with the sauce.

WHOLE FISH WITH FIVE SHREDS IN HOT SAUCE

1 1 kg (2 lb) fresh perch, bream, or red snapper

3 dried black mushrooms, soaked for 25 minutes

15 g (½ oz) Chinese pickles

30 g (1 oz) canned bamboo shoots, drained

1 small green capsicum (bell pepper)

3 spring onions (scallions), trimmed
and shredded

3 thick slices fresh ginger, shredded

¼ cup (2 fl oz) frying oil

white pepper

Seasoning:

½ teaspoon salt

1 spring onion (scallion), trimmed and shredded

2 slices fresh ginger, shredded

1 tablespoon softened lard or frying oil

Sauce:

⅓ cup chicken stock

¼ cup (2 fl oz) white vinegar

¼ cup (2 fl oz) tomato sauce (ketchup)

1½ teaspoons salt

⅓ cup sugar

½ teaspoon finely chopped garlic

½-1 teaspoon chilli oil

1½ teaspoons cornflour (cornstarch)

Place fish in a large wok. Add seasoning ingredients and water to cover. Cover wok and bring just to the boil, reduce heat and poach for 15 minutes, or until just cooked through. Test by inserting a fork into thickest part of fish. Drain and transfer to a serving plate.

Squeeze excess water from mushrooms and remove stems. Shred the caps. Cut pickles, bamboo shoots, and pepper into matchstick strips.

Arrange spring onions and ginger on the fish. Drain liquid from wok, wipe out and heat oil to piping hot. Pour half over the fish. Fry shredded ingredients in remaining oil for 2 minutes, stirring occasionally. Add pre-mixed sauce and bring to the boil. Simmer for 2 minutes, then pour over fish and season generously with white pepper. Serve.

STIR-FRIED SQUID WITH VEGETABLES

	Seasoning/Sauce:
625 g (1¼ lb) fresh squid	
30 g (1 oz) canned bamboo shoots, drained and sliced	¼ cup (2 fl oz) chicken stock
	½ teaspoon sesame oil (optional)
1 medium carrot, peeled and thinly sliced	1 teaspoon salt
12 snow peas, strings removed*	½ teaspoon m.s.g. (optional)
5 cups (1¼ litres) deep-frying oil	½ teaspoon sugar
1½ spring onions (scallions), trimmed and sliced	¼ teaspoon ground black pepper
	1 teaspoon cornflour (cornstarch)

Remove heads and stomachs from squid and discard. Pull away the pink skin with fins attached, leaving only the white tubular bodies. Cut open and press out flat. Rinse well, pulling away any white membrane. Score on the inside in a close diagonal criss-cross pattern, cutting at a slight angle.

Cut into diamond-shaped bite-sized pieces and blanch for 10 seconds in boiling water, then drain well. Blanch bamboo shoots, carrots, and snow peas or other vegetables and drain well.

Heat oil to moderate and fry squid in a basket for 20 seconds only. Lift out and drain well. Pour off all but ⅓ cup of oil and stir-fry spring onions, ginger, and garlic on fairly high heat for 45 seconds. Add vegetables and stir-fry together until beginning to soften, about 1 minute.

Pour in pre-mixed seasoning/sauce and bring to the boil. Simmer briefly, return squid and heat through. Transfer to a serving plate.

Do not overcook or the squid will become tough and chewy.

* Or use 1 small green capsicum pepper, cut into small squares, 12 broccoli or cauliflower florets, or 6 soaked dried black mushrooms.

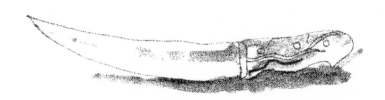

BAKED STUFFED MANDARIN FISH

1 750 g (1½ lb) Mandarin fish (perch or trout)	**Seasoning B:**
3 thick slices fresh ginger, shredded	⅓ teaspoon salt
75 g (2½ oz) fatty pork, minced (ground)	½ teaspoon m.s.g. (optional)
30 g (1 oz) blanched almonds, toasted and chopped	¼ teaspoon white pepper
30 g (1 oz) duck or chicken liver, diced	1 teaspoon rice wine or dry sherry
15 g (1 oz) canned water chestnuts, drained and diced	1 tablespoon chicken stock
1½ spring onions (scallions), trimmed and diced	2 teaspoons cornflour (cornstarch)
cornflour (cornstarch)	**Sauce:**
2 tablespoons frying oil	1 cup (8 fl oz) chicken stock
Seasoning A:	2 tablespoons light soy sauce
¼ teaspoon white pepper	2 teaspoons rice wine or dry sherry
1 tablespoon light soy sauce	1 teaspoon sesame oil
2 teaspoons rice wine or dry sherry	½ teaspoon salt
¾ teaspoon sesame oil	¼ teaspoon m.s.g. (optional)
	½ teaspoon sugar

Scale and clean the fish and carefully cut away the backbone with a thick layer of meat attached to it. Rub the fish inside and out with the seasoning A and half the ginger. Leave for 10 minutes.

Scrape the fish from bones and mix with pork, almonds, livers, water chestnuts, spring onions, remaining ginger, and seasoning B. Wipe out fish, dust lightly with cornflour and fill with prepared stuffing. Stand fish on its stomach on a greased baking tray or sew up the opening and cook on its side, turning once.

Pour pre-mixed sauce over fish, add 2 tablespoons of frying oil and bake in a preheated low oven at 120°C (250°F/Gas ½) until golden and cooked through, about 40 minutes. Baste frequently with sauce during cooking to prevent fish drying out.

Carefully transfer to a serving plate and garnish with additional shredded onion and ginger. Serve at once.

SCALLOPS WITH SHRIMPS
AND MUSHROOMS

12 large fresh sea scallops	**Seasoning A:**
155 g (5 oz) raw peeled shrimps	½ teaspoon salt
90 g (3 oz) canned straw mushrooms, drained and cut in halves	2 teaspoons ginger wine
	Seasoning B:
¼ cup (2 fl oz) frying oil	⅓ teaspoon salt
2 spring onions (scallions, trimmed and sliced)	¾ teaspoon sugar
3 slices fresh ginger	½ cup (4 fl oz) chicken stock
cornflour (cornstarch)	
2 egg whites, well beaten	

Place scallops in a dish and add seasoning A. De-vein shrimps, rinse with cold water and add to scallops. Leave to marinate for 10 minutes.

Bring seasoning B to the boil in a small saucepan. Add mushrooms and simmer for 3 minutes. Remove from heat and leave in stock.

Heat oil and sauté spring onions and ginger until softened, then add scallops and shrimps and sauté on moderately high heat until barely cooked through. The scallops should be white and just firm, the shrimps pink and firm.

Add the mushrooms and stock and bring to the boil. Mix a little cornflour with cold water and pour into sauce. Simmer until thickened, then slowly drizzle in beaten egg whites and cook without stirring until egg sets in white strands in sauce.

SWEETENED SOY SAUCE

2 tablespoons dark soy sauce	1¼ tablespoons malt sugar
2 tablespoons sugar	2 teaspoons sesame oil

Mix all ingredients, stirring until sugar has completely dissolved. Excellent with fish, prawn, and crab.

SMOKED POMFRET

1 700 g (1⅓ lb) pomfret or John Dory	**Sauce:**
½ cup green tea leaves*	¼ cup (2 fl oz) chicken stock
2 tablespoons sugar	2 teaspoons light soy sauce
Seasoning:	½ teaspoon rice wine or dry sherry
¼ teaspoon salt	½ teaspoon m.s.g. (optional)
1 tablespoon sugar	½ teaspoon sugar
¼ cup (2 fl oz) light soy sauce	½ teaspoon sesame oil
1 tablespoon rice wine or dry sherry	½ teaspoon cornflour (cornstarch)
4 spring onions (scallions), trimmed and sliced	
4 slices fresh ginger, shredded	

Cut fish in halves at an angle from front of top fin to behind lower fin. Mix seasoning ingredients and pour over fish. Leave for one hour to marinate.

Brush a cake-cooling rack with oil and place fish on this. Set in a baking tray containing tea leaves and sugar and place in a preheated hot oven at 230°C (450°F/Gas 8). Bake for 25 minutes, turning once.

Bring sauce ingredients to the boil and pour over fish just before serving. This fish is now frequently served with mayonnaise.

* Or use pine wood chips.

STEWED RIVER EEL WITH DICED PORK AND MUSHROOMS

1 750 g (1½ lb) fresh-water eel	**Seasoning A:**
6 cups (1½ litres) deep-frying oil	¾ teaspoon salt
125 g (4 oz) fatty or roast pork, diced	¼ cup (2 fl oz) light soy sauce
8 cloves garlic	1½ teaspoons dark soy sauce
3 pieces dried orange peel	1½ tablespoons rice wine or dry sherry
4 spring onions (scallions), trimmed and cut in halves	**Seasoning B/Sauce:**
	2 tablespoons light soy sauce
5 slices fresh ginger	1 tablespoon sugar
6 dried black mushrooms, soaked for 25 minutes	¾ teaspoon m.s.g. (optional)
3 cups (24 fl oz) chicken stock	pinch of white pepper
cornflour (cornstarch)	
sesame oil	
white pepper	

Wash eels, rubbing with salt to remove slime. Rinse in cold water and cut into 5 cm (2 in) pieces, discarding the head and tail. Blanch in boiling water for 1 minute, drain and place in a dish with seasoning A. Leave for 20 minutes. Drain, reserving the marinade.

Heat deep-frying oil and fry pork until lightly coloured. Drain and set aside. Add eel and deep-fry for 1 minute, drain and transfer to a casserole. Scatter diced pork on top. Drain off all but ⅓ cup of oil and fry garlic and orange peel for 1 minute, place with the eel, then fry spring onions, ginger and drained mushrooms briefly and transfer, with the oil, to a casserole.

Add reserved marinade and seasoning B/sauce. Heat stock to boiling and pour over eel. Cover and simmer until eel is tender, about 30 minutes. Strain sauce into wok and bring to the boil, simmer until well reduced, then thicken with cornflour mixed with a little cold water and check seasoning. Pour over eel and season with a dash of sesame oil and white pepper. Serve in the casserole.

Lobster with Black Beans and Chillis (recipe page 22)

CHARCOAL ROASTED EEL
ON SKEWERS

Serve as an appetiser or main dish

1 750 g (1½ lb) fresh-water eel	**Seasoning:**
2 tablespoons frying oil	3 tablespoons finely chopped spring onion (scallion)
1½ teaspoons sesame oil (optional)	
	1 tablespoon grated fresh ginger
	¼ cup (2 fl oz) light soy sauce
	1 tablespoon dark soy sauce
	2 tablespoons rice wine or dry sherry
	juice of 1 lemon
	2 tablespoons vegetable oil
	½ teaspoon m.s.g. (optional)
	2 tablespoons sugar
	⅓ teaspoon ground black pepper

Clean the eel, cut off head and tail section and discard. Cut body into pieces about 4 cm (1⅔ in) long and cut down to backbone so pieces can be pressed out flat.

Place on a tray and pour on seasoning ingredients. Leave for 10 minutes, then turn and leave for a further 10 minutes. Thread each piece onto two metal skewers, passing across pieces so they remain flat.

Place eel on an oiled grid, skin side downwards over glowing charcoal, and grill (broil) for 3 minutes. Turn and cook the other side for 2 minutes. Brush with any remaining marinade and continue to cook and turn until evenly cooked with the outside crisp, dark, and glazed with sauce, the meat inside, moist and white. Do not overcook.

Serve on a bed of shredded lettuce.

Meat

PORK AND DUCK LIVER ROLL

Serve as an appetiser or main dish

280 g (9 oz) lean pork, finely minced (ground)	**Seasoning:**
60 g (2 oz) canned water chestnuts, drained and finely chopped	1 egg white, beaten
	¾ teaspoon salt
1 duck (or chicken) liver, cubed	½ teaspoon m.s.g. (optional)
1 small onion, diced	1 tablespoon light soy sauce
185 g (6 oz) pork omentum*	1 teaspoon rice wine or dry sherry
1 egg white, beaten	2 teaspoons cornflour (cornstarch)
1 tablespoon cornflour (cornstarch)	
4 cups (1 litre) deep-frying oil	

Mix pork and water chestnuts with seasoning ingredients and set aside. Use a little oil to sauté liver and diced onion, then add to pork mixture.

Wash pork omentum and spread on a board. It may be easier to work if divided into several even-sized squares. If using the chicken skin, cut in halves for easier handling. Make a paste of egg white and cornflour and spread over pork fat or beancurd skin. Omit if using chicken skin. Spread on pork mixture, leaving a wide border all round. Roll into a long sausage shape and stick down ends and long edge with more egg white paste. The chicken skin rolls should be secured with toothpicks or sewn up with a needle and thread.

Heat oil to moderate and fry roll(s) until cooked through, and crisp and golden, about 4 minutes. Remove from oil and drain well. Cut diagonally across rolls into thick slices and arrange on a serving plate. Serve with sweet and sour sauce or with spiced salt.

* If pork omentum (caul net/fat) is unobtainable, use either a dampened sheet of beancurd skin or a chicken skin.

SLOW-COOKED CORNED PORK

	Seasoning:
1¼ kg (2½ lb) pork shoulder (butt)	1 tablespoon rice wine or dry sherry
1 tablespoon saltpetre	3 spring onions (scallions), trimmed
	1½ teaspoons grated fresh ginger
	1½ teaspoons salt
	2 star anise
	2 teaspoons Chinese brown peppercorns
	5 cm (2 in) piece cinnamon stick

Blanch pork in boiling water, then place in a pan with water to cover and add saltpetre. Leave, covered, for 2 hours. Blanch again in boiling water and rinse in cold water. Drain well. Place pork with seasoning ingredients in a heavy saucepan and add water to cover. Bring to the boil, reduce heat and simmer for 2½ hours, turning often. Remove from heat and leave to cool in pot. Remove meat when cool, slice thinly and arrange on a serving plate. Pour a little of the sauce over top.

DEEP-FRIED PORK CHOPS

	Seasoning:
6 small pork loin chops (about 700 g/1⅓ lb)	½ teaspoon salt
cornflour (cornstarch)	¾ teaspoon m. s. g. (optional)
2 eggs, well beaten	1 tablespoon rice wine or dry sherry
1½ cups dry breadcrumbs	1 tablespoon finely chopped spring onion
6 cups (1½ litres) deep-frying oil	1½ teaspoons grated fresh ginger
spiced salt	
Worcestershire or light soy sauce	

Bat the meaty centres of the chops with side of a cleaver to flatten and tenderise. Rub on seasoning ingredients and leave for 25 minutes to marinate.

Dust pork chops lightly with cornflour, then dip into beaten egg and coat thickly with breadcrumbs on both sides.

Heat oil to fairly hot and fry pork chops for 1 minute. Lower heat cook until chops are well browned and cooked through, about 3 minutes longer.

Drain well and serve with dips of spiced salt and Worcestershire or soy sauce.

CANTONESE ROAST PORK

Serve hot or cold as an appetiser or main dish

1 kg (2 lb) pork fillet (tenderloin)	**Seasoning:**
1 tablespoon five spice powder	½ cup (4 fl oz) light soy sauce
2 teaspoons finely ground Chinese brown peppercorns	2½ tablespoons soybean paste, dark soy sauce or oyster sauce
3 tablespoons finely chopped spring onion (scallion)	1 tablespoon sesame oil
	2 tablespoons rice wine or dry sherry
1 tablespoon finely chopped fresh ginger	⅓ cup sugar
	red food colouring

Special Equipment: A rotisserie oven or metal hooks for hanging meat in the oven.

Choose large fillets and cut lengthwise into two or three strips, about 15 cm (6 in) long and 5 cm (2 in) wide. Rub with five spice powder and ground peppercorns and place in a dish. Arrange chopped spring onion and ginger on top, then pour on the pre-mixed seasoning after stirring until the sugar dissolves. (Add red food colouring to give a fairly bright colour.) Cover dish with plastic wrap and leave for about 4 hours to marinate.

If oven has a rotisserie, thread strips of meat through one end onto spike so that they hang down in oven. Place a drip tray underneath. Otherwise, secure each strip by one end on metal hooks. Position one rack on the highest setting in oven and remove other racks. Hang hooks on this rack, separating each piece as much as possible.

Do not set rotisserie in motion. Cook pork on very high heat for the first 10 minutes, about 240°C (450°F/Gas 8) then reduce to around 170°C (325-350°F/Gas 3-4) to cook for a further 20 minutes. Brush frequently with pan drippings to keep meat moist and to glaze surface.

When done, leave to cool slightly, then slice and serve with hot mustard and light soy sauce as dips. Use in recipes requiring barbecue or roast pork and in assortments of cold cuts as an appetiser.

STEWED PORK WITH FERMENTED BEANCURD AND TARO

750 g (1½ lb) 'five flowered' pork (belly/fresh bacon) *	**Seasoning B:**
1 tablespoon dark soy sauce	1½ teaspoons salt
6 cups (1½ litres) deep-frying oil	2 teaspoons sugar
185 g (6 oz) fresh taro, yam, or sweet potato	¼ cup (2 fl oz) light soy sauce
4 cups (1 litre) chicken stock	2 teaspoons dark soy sauce
cornflour (cornstarch)	1 tablespoon rice wine or dry sherry
Seasoning A:	
2 tablespoons finely chopped spring onion (scallion)	
2 teaspoons finely chopped fresh ginger	
1½ teaspoons finely chopped garlic	
4 cubes fermented beancurd with the liquid, mashed	

Wipe pork and blanch in boiling water for 2 minutes, then remove and leave to dry. Rub with dark soy sauce and deep-fry in hot oil until well coloured on the surface, about 5 minutes. Drain well.

Peel taro and cut into cubes. Deep-fry until lightly coloured, about 2 minutes. Drain. Cut pork into the same sized pieces.

Pour off most of the oil, retaining about 2 tablespoons. Fry seasoning A ingredients for 2 minutes, adding a little chicken stock to prevent them sticking to pan. Add seasoning B and cook briefly, then pour in chicken stock and bring to the boil. Reduce heat and add pork. Simmer for about 30 minutes, then add taro and cook until both pork and taro are tender.

Transfer meat and vegetables to a serving plate. Return about 1 cupful of sauce to the boil and thicken with a paste of cornflour and cold water. Pour over dish and serve.

* Or use a less fatty cut, if preferred.

PORK FILLET ROLLS IN SWEET AND SOUR SAUCE

375 g (12 oz) pork fillet (tenderloin)	**Seasoning B/Sauce:**
cornflour (cornstarch)	2 tablespoons finely chopped spring onion (scallion)
3 cups (24 fl oz) deep-frying oil	
1 small carrot, diced and parboiled	2 teaspoons finely chopped fresh ginger
1 small cucumber, diced	¼ cup (2 fl oz) chicken stock or cold water
30 g (1 oz) canned bamboo shoots, drained and diced	¼ cup (2 fl oz) tomato sauce (ketchup)
	2 tablespoons white vinegar
1 medium brown onion, diced	2¾ tablespoons sugar
Seasoning A:	½ teaspoon salt
½ teaspoon salt	1 teaspoon cornflour (cornstarch)
¾ teaspoon m.s.g. (optional)	
¼ teaspoon white pepper	
2 teaspoons rice wine or dry sherry	
1 teaspoon sesame oil (optional)	

Thinly slice pork, then score on one side in a criss-cross pattern and cut into 5 cm (2 in) squares. Mix with seasoning A and leave for 20 minutes. Coat pork lightly with cornflour, roll each piece and deep-fry in smoking oil for 1 minute. Remove and drain well. Turn heat to moderate and return pork. Cook for about 2 minutes more, until cooked through and golden brown. Remove and keep warm.

Pour off oil, wipe out wok and return 3 tablespoons of oil. Reheat to moderate and stir-fry diced vegetables for 2 minutes, then add chopped spring onion and ginger and stir-fry for 30 seconds. Pour in remaining pre-mixed seasoning B/sauce and bring to the boil. Simmer for 2½ minutes, then add pork and stir until the meat is evenly glazed with sauce. Serve.

STIR-FRIED PORK WITH SPRING ONIONS IN SOY SAUCE

250 g (8 oz) pork fillet (tenderloin)	**Seasoning B:**
2 large spring onions (scallions)	2 teaspoons dark soy sauce
1/4 cup (2 fl oz) frying oil	1/2 teaspoon m.s.g. (optional)
1 thick slice fresh ginger, shredded	1/4 teaspoon ground black pepper
1/2 teaspoon crushed garlic	1/2 teaspoon sugar
2 teaspoons rice wine or dry sherry	
2 tablespoons light soy sauce	
Seasoning A:	
2 teaspoons sugar	
1 tablespoon light soy sauce	
2 teaspoons rice wine or dry sherry	
2 teaspoons cornflour (cornstarch)	

Very thinly slice the pork across the grain, then place in a dish with the seasoning A, mix well and leave for 30 minutes.

Cut spring onions in halves lengthwise and cut into 4 cm (1⅔ in) pieces. Heat oil in a wok and stir-fry spring onions, ginger and garlic for 1 minute. Add pork and stir-fry on high heat until lightly coloured, 1½-2 minutes.

Sizzle wine and soy sauce onto sides of pan and stir in, then add seasoning B and mix thoroughly.

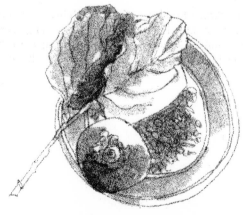

SWEET AND SOUR PORK RIBS

500 g (1 lb) meaty pork ribs or chops	**Sauce:**
1 small green capsicum (bell pepper)	⅓ cup liquid from canned pineapple
1 small red capsicum (bell pepper)	⅓ cup white vinegar
2 slices canned pineapple, drained	2 tablespoons tomato sauce (ketchup)
1 small white onion	1 tablespoon vegetable oil
7 cups (1¾ litres) deep-frying oil	2½ tablespoons sugar
1 small carrot, sliced and parboiled	½ teaspoon salt
cornflour (cornstarch)	pinch of ground black pepper
	½-¾ teaspoon finely chopped garlic
	2 teaspoons cornflour (cornstarch)

Cut pork ribs or chops into 2.5 cm (1 in) cubes. Wash peppers and cut in halves, remove stems, seed cores, and inner white ribs. Cut into quarters. Cut pineapple into pieces the same size as peppers. Peel onion and cut into quarters, cutting from stem to root. Trim away the base to allow pieces to separate.

Pour about 1½ cups of cornflour into a paper or plastic bag and add meat. Close bag and shake vigorously to thickly coat meat with flour. Empty into a colander and shake off excess flour.

Heat oil to fairly hot. Fry pork, about 10 pieces at a time, until well browned and crisp on the surface, about 3 minutes. Drain and keep oil warm.

Transfer 2-3 tablespoons of oil to another wok and fry onion for 30 seconds. Add the peppers and fry a further 30 seconds, then add the carrots and stir-fry the vegetables together for a further 1 minute. Pour in pre-mixed sauce and bring to the boil. Simmer for 2 minutes, then add pineapple.

Reheat oil and fry pork for a second time until crisp, about 1 minute. Drain and transfer to sauce. Stir until evenly glazed with sauce, then serve.

SWEET AND SPICY SPARE RIBS

18 American-style pork spare ribs
(about 700 g/1⅓ lb) *

Seasoning:

¼ teaspoon salt
1½ tablespoons sugar
2 teaspoons five spice powder
2 tablespoons light soy sauce
2 tablespoons rice wine or dry sherry
2 tablespoons soy bean paste
2 cubes fermented beancurd with the liquid, mashed
2 tablespoons vegetables oil
1½ teaspoons crushed garlic

Mix seasoning ingredients together. Place ribs in a dish and smear thickly on both sides with seasoning paste. Leave for 1½-2 hours to absorb flavourings, then arrange on an oiled oven tray and roast in a preheated moderately hot oven 220°C (425°F/Gas 7) or under slow grill for about 25 minutes.

Turn ribs occasionally during cooking and brush with any remaining seasoning paste and pan drippings. Add a little vegetable oil if they begin to dry.

Serve with spiced salt (page 14) as a dip and with plum sauce.

* Pork rib bones with a spare covering of meat. If unobtainable use small pork chops.

PORK RIBS WITH BLACK BEAN SAUCE

6 meaty pork ribs (about 625 g/1¼ lb)	1 teaspoon dark soy sauce
1½ tablespoons fermented black beans	2 teaspoons dry sherry
¾ teaspoon crushed garlic	2 tablespoons water
1½ teaspoons sugar	1 tablespoon vegetable oil
2 tablespoons light soy sauce	1 fresh red chilli pepper (optional)

Trim ribs and cut into 5 or 6 pieces each. Wash black beans and dry well. Chop coarsely and mix with remaining ingredients. Place ribs in a dish and cover with prepared seasonings. Leave for 1-2 hours to absorb flavourings.

Set dish on a rack and steam over gently boiling water until pork is completely tender, about 1 hour. Serve in the dish. If using the chilli pepper, add before steaming.

STEAMED PORK WITH CARROTS AND MUSHROOMS

	Seasoning:
500 g (1 lb) lean pork, from the upper leg	1/4 cup (2 fl oz) light soy sauce
1 medium to large carrot	2 teaspoons rice wine or dry sherry
2 spring onions (scallions), trimmed and cut in halves	1/2 teaspoon salt
3 slices fresh ginger	1 teaspoon sugar
90 g (3 oz) canned champignons, drained	1/2 teaspoon m.s.g. (optional)
	1/4 teaspoon ground Chinese brown peppercorns

Trim any fat from meat and cut into 2 cm (3/4 in) cubes. Peel carrot and cut into small cubes. Place half the pork in a dish and add half the onion and a piece of ginger. Layer carrot, champignons, and remaining pork on top and add remaining onion and ginger.

Mix seasoning and pour evenly over dish, then add chicken stock or water to barely cover the top layer.

Set dish on a rack and steam over rapidly boiling water until tender, about 1 1/4 hours.

Strain liquid into wok and check seasonings. Thicken with a thin solution of cornflour and cold water and stir well. Pour over dish and serve.

For dramatic presentation, arrange the ingredients alternately in a sunburst design in a large round dish.

'SU TUNG PO' PORK

825 g (1 3/4 lb) 'five flowered' pork (belly/fresh bacon)	2 spring onions (scallions), cut in halves
1 tablespoon salt	4 thick slices fresh ginger, bruised
8 pieces rock candy (or 1/2 cup crystal sugar)	90 g (3 oz) champignons, sliced
1/3 cup light soy sauce	8 dried black mushrooms, soaked for 25 minutes then drained
1/4 cup (2 fl oz) rice wine or dry sherry	

Rub salt over pork, leave for 1 hour, blanch in boiling water for 2 minutes and rinse in cold water. Sear in a hot dry pan until crisp. Slice 1 cm (1/3 in) thick, then into strips 5 cm (2 in) wide. Simmer with remaining ingredients in a covered pot for 2 1/2-3 hours. Remove meat and mushrooms, discard onion and ginger, bring sauce to the boil and strain over meat.

CHINESE PEPPER — SALT

1½ tablespoons Chinese brown peppercorns	4 tablespoons table salt

Dry-fry peppercorns in a wok over low to moderate heat until aromatic, about 3 minutes, stirring constantly. Grind to a fine powder then return to wok with salt and dry-fry together, turning constantly with a wok spatula until thoroughly mixed and aromatic. Do not allow salt to colour. Cool, then store in an airtight jar.

STEAMED BEEF MEATBALLS AND SPINACH ON RICE

1¼ cups raw short grain white rice	**Seasoning:**
375 g (12 oz) lean beef, finely minced (ground)	1¼ teaspoons salt
60 g (2 oz) pork fat, coarsely minced (ground)	½ teaspoon sugar
2 tablespoons finely chopped spring onion (scallion)	1 tablespoon light soy sauce
	2 tablespoons cold water
1¼ teaspoons finely chopped fresh ginger	1 tablespoon frying oil
60 g (2 oz) canned water chestnuts or bamboo shoots, finely diced	2 teaspoons cornflour (cornstarch)
250 g (8 oz) fresh spinach leaves (collard greens)	

Soak rice in cold water. Mix beef and pork fat together and add seasoning ingredients. Knead into a smooth paste and leave for at least 1 hour, then add remaining ingredients, except spinach.

Drain rice and pour into a saucepan. Add 1 teaspoon salt and water to cover by 2.5 cm (1 in). Cook, covered, until water level recedes below rice, then arrange well-washed spinach leaves on top.

Form meat paste into large meatballs and place on spinach leaves. Continue to cook on very low heat until rice is tender and fluffy and the meatballs cooked through, about 12 minutes.

Transfer meatballs and vegetables to one serving plate. Stir up rice and serve into rice bowls or a separate serving plate and serve with meatballs.

STIR-FRIED BEEF WITH YOUNG GINGER AND PINEAPPLE

250 g (8 oz) beef fillet (tenderloin)	**Seasoning A:**
45 g (1½ oz) canned pineapple pieces, drained	1 egg white, beaten
2 cm (¾ in) piece fresh young ginger*	½ teaspoon salt
¼ cup (2 fl oz) frying oil	2 teaspoons vegetable oil
1 spring onion (scallion), trimmed and sliced	2 teaspoons cornflour (cornstarch)
2 teaspoons rice wine or dry sherry	**Seasoning B/Sauce:**
	2 tablespoons chicken stock
	1 tablespoon light soy sauce
	⅓ teaspoon salt
	½ teaspoon sugar
	½ teaspoon cornflour (cornstarch)

Partially freeze beef and cut across grain into paper-thin slices, then cut into strips about 2.5 x 5 cm (1 x 2 in). Place in a dish with the seasoning A and leave to marinate for 20 minutes.

Cut each of the pineapple pieces in halves. Peel and very thinly slice ginger. Heat oil in a wok and stir-fry spring onion and ginger for 1 minute, then push to one side of pan and add beef. Stir-fry until it changes colour, then sizzle in wine and add pre-mixed seasoning B/sauce. Simmer for 1 minute, then add pineapple and heat through.

* For a milder taste, blanch the sliced ginger before use.

BEEF IN OYSTER SAUCE

250 g (8 oz) beef steak (fillet/tenderloin or rump)	**Seasoning B/Sauce:**
280 g (9 oz) Chinese (celery) cabbage	2 tablespoons chicken stock
6 dried black mushrooms, soaked for 25 minutes	1½ teaspoons dark soy sauce
¼ cup (2 fl oz) frying oil	1 tablespoon light soy sauce
Seasoning A:	1 tablespoon rice wine or dry sherry
½ teaspoon salt	½ teaspoon salt
1½ teaspoons sugar	1 teaspoon sugar
½ teaspoon m.s.g. (optional)	½ teaspoon cornflour (cornstarch)
¼ teaspoon white pepper	2 tablespoons oyster sauce
1 tablespoon water	
2 teaspoons dark soy sauce	
2 teaspoons rice wine or dry sherry	
1 tablespoon vegetable oil	
2 teaspoons cornflour (cornstarch)	

Partially freeze beef and cut into very thin slices, then into narrow strips. Place in a dish with the seasoning A mix well and leave for 45 minutes to marinate.

Wash cabbage and cut into 5 cm (2 in) pieces. Simmer in lightly salted water for 3 minutes and drain well. Drain mushrooms, remove stems and simmer mushroom caps in a little chicken stock or water for 10 minutes, adding a dash each of salt, sugar, and pepper. Remove from heat and leave in liquid until needed.

Heat oil in a wok and stir-fry beef on very high heat until it changes colour. Remove. Add cabbage and stir-fry briefly, then add mushrooms and pre-mixed seasoning B/sauce except oyster sauce. Simmer until thickened.

Return beef and stir in oyster sauce. Heat through and serve.

FILLET OF BEEF WITH SALTED MUSTARD GREENS AND BLACK BEAN SAUCE

250 g (8 oz) beef fillet (tenderloin)	**Seasoning B/Sauce:**
30 g (1 oz) salted mustard root	2 tablespoons chicken stock
1 tablespoon fermented black beans	1/4 teaspoon salt
3/4 teaspoon finely chopped garlic	1/2 teaspoon sugar
3/4 teaspoon sugar	1/2 teaspoon m. s. g. (optional)
3 cups (24 fl oz) deep-frying oil or use 1/3 cup frying oil	1/4 teaspoon ground black pepper (optional)
	1/2 teaspoon sesame oil (optional)
2 teaspoons rice wine or dry sherry	3/4 teaspoon cornflour (cornstarch)
1 tablespoon light soy sauce	
Seasoning A:	
1/2 teaspoon salt	
1/4 teaspoon m. s. g. (optional)	
1/4 teaspoon bicarbonate of soda (optional)	
1 1/4 teaspoons sugar	
2 tablespoons water	
1 1/2 tablespoons vegetable oil	
2 teaspoons cornflour (cornstarch)	

Partially freeze the beef, cut into very thin slices across the grain and then cut each piece into three. Add seasoning A ingredients, except cornflour and leave for 15 minutes, then add cornflour, mix in and leave a further 10 minutes.

Soak mustard root or other pickled vegetables in cold water for 20 minutes, drain well and squeeze out excess water. Cut into small dice. Wash black beans and dry well, chop and mix with garlic and sugar.

Heat deep-frying oil in a wok to smoking point and fry the beef in a frying basket for 30 seconds. Or stir-fry in frying oil on very high heat for 1 minute. Remove and drain well. Keep warm. Pour off all but 2 tablespoons oil and add black bean mixture. Stir-fry for 30 seconds, then add mustard or pickled vegetables and stir-fry for 30 seconds longer. Sizzle wine and soy sauce onto sides of pan and stir in.

Add the pre-mixed seasoning B/sauce and bring to the boil. Return beef and heat through, then serve.

STIR-FRIED BEEF WITH GREEN AND RED PEPPERS

185 g (6 oz) beef fillet (tenderloin)	**Seasoning B/Sauce:**
1 medium green capsicum (bell pepper)	1/4 cup (2 fl oz) chicken stock or water
1-2 fresh red chilli peppers	1/2 teaspoon sesame oil
1/3 cup frying oil	1/2 teaspoon salt
1 large spring onion (scallion), trimmed and sliced	1/4 teaspoon m.s.g. (optional)
	1/2 teaspoon sugar
1 1/2 teaspoons finely chopped fresh ginger	1/4 teaspoon ground black pepper
1 1/2 teaspoons finely chopped garlic	1 teaspoon cornflour (cornstarch)
1 tablespoon fermented black beans, or use hot black bean sauce	
1 1/2 teaspoons rice wine or dry sherry	
Seasoning A:	
1/4 teaspoon m.s.g. (optional)	
1 tablespoon light soy sauce	
2 teaspoons rice wine or dry sherry	
1 tablespoon frying oil	
1 tablespoon cold water	
2 teaspoons cornflour (cornstarch)	

Partially freeze beef then cut into paper-thin slices across grain and into fine shreds. Place beef shreds in a dish with the seasoning A, mix well and leave for 25 minutes. Cut open green pepper and red chillies and remove stems, seed-cores, and inner white ribs. Cut into shreds.

Heat oil and stir-fry beef until it changes colour, then remove from oil and keep warm. Add onion, ginger, and garlic to pan and stir-fry for 45 seconds. Push to one side of pan and add capsicum and chilli peppers. Stir-fry until softened, splashing in about 1 1/2 tablespoons of cold water to soften the peppers. When liquid dries up, add chopped black beans or black bean sauce and fry briefly, then return meat and sizzle wine onto sides of pan and stir in.

Add pre-mixed seasoning B/sauce and stir on high heat until thickened. Transfer to a serving plate.

Egg Custard (recipe page 71) and
Sweet Rice Balls in Red Bean Soup (recipe page 70)

RAINBOW BEEF IN LETTUCE LEAVES

155 g (5 oz) beef fillet (tenderloin)	**Seasoning:**
60 g (2 oz) canned bamboo shoots, drained	¼ teaspoon salt
60 g (2 oz) fresh celery	½ teaspoon sugar
1 small carrot	1 teaspoon light soy sauce
1 small green capsicum (bell pepper)	1 teaspoon rice wine or dry sherry
1 fresh red chilli pepper	1½ teaspoons vegetable oil
3 dried black mushrooms, soaked for 25 minutes	1 tablespoon cold water
6 cups (1½ litres) deep-frying oil	1 teaspoon cornflour (cornstarch)
45 g (1½ oz) rice vermicelli	
12 fresh lettuce leaf cups	

Thinly slice beef, then cut into fine shreds. Place in a dish with the seasoning ingredients, mix well and leave for 1 hour. Cut vegetables into fine shreds.

Heat oil to smoking point. Break rice vermicelli into small pieces and place in a frying basket. Deep-fry for about 20 seconds until it expands and turns crisp. Drain and place on a serving plate.

Pour off all but 2½ tablespoons of oil and fry meat until it changes colour, then push to one side of wok and add shredded vegetables. Stir-fry until softened but retaining crispness, about 2 minutes, then stir in beef and spoon onto rice vermicelli.

Wash lettuce leaves and place on a serving plate. To eat, spoon a portion of meat, vegetables, and noodles into lettuce leaf and roll up. *Hoisin* or plum sauce can be served as a dip.

Rainbow Beef in Lettuce Leaves

BEEF FU YUNG

90 g (3 oz) beef fillet (tenderloin)	**Seasoning B/Sauce:**
4 eggs, beaten	¼ cup (2 fl oz) chicken stock
2 egg whites, well beaten	2 teaspoons light soy sauce
2 teaspoons cornflour (cornstarch)	1 tablespoon oyster sauce
1 tablespoon water	1 teaspoon rice wine or dry sherry
¼ teaspoon salt	⅓ teaspoon sugar
1 teaspoon sesame oil	1 tablespoon frying oil
2 tablespoons frying oil	½ teaspoon cornflour (cornstarch)
2 spring onions (scallions), trimmed and shredded	
1 slice fresh ginger, shredded	
Seasoning A:	
⅓ teaspoon salt	
¼ teaspoon m.s.g. (optional)	
2 teaspoons light soy sauce	
1 teaspoon rice wine or dry sherry	
1½ teaspoons cornflour (cornstarch)	

Partially freeze beef, cut into very thin slices across grain, then into long thin shreds. Mix with seasoning A and leave for 15 minutes to marinate.

Mix eggs, egg whites, cornflour, water and salt together, beat for 1 minute, then set aside.

Heat sesame oil and frying oil together in a wok and sauté spring onions and ginger for 30 seconds. Push to one side of pan and add shredded beef. Sauté on high heat until meat changes colour, then reduce heat to moderate.

Pour in egg mixture and cook until underside is lightly coloured and firm. Cut into quarters and turn each piece. Cook until omelette is just done right through. Do not allow to dry out. Transfer to a warmed serving plate and keep warm.

Wipe out wok and add pre-mixed seasoning B/sauce. Bring to the boil and simmer until thickened. Pour over omelette and serve immediately.

CANTONESE BEEF STEAKS

500 g (1 lb) beef fillet (tenderloin)

1/3 cup frying oil

2 spring onions (scallions), trimmed and shredded

2 slices fresh ginger, shredded

2-3 cloves garlic, thinly sliced

Seasoning A:

1/2 teaspoon salt

1/2 teaspoon m.s.g. (optional)

1/4 teaspoon bicarbonate of soda (optional)

1/2 teaspoon sugar

1 teaspoon dark soy sauce

2 teaspoons rice wine or dry sherry

1 tablespoon cold water

2 teaspoons cornflour (cornstarch)

Seasoning B/Sauce:

1/3 cup chicken stock

2 teaspoons dark soy sauce

2 teaspoons light soy sauce

2 teaspoons Worcestershire sauce

1 tablespoon barbecue sauce or soybean paste

1 tablespoon tomato sauce (ketchup)

2 teaspoons rice wine or dry sherry

2 teaspoons sugar

1 teaspoon cornflour (cornstarch)

1/4 teaspoon salt

1/4 teaspoon white pepper

Chill meat, then cut into thin steaks across grain. Place in a dish and add pre-mixed seasoning A. Rub into meat and leave for 10 minutes, then turn and marinate for a further 10 minutes.

Heat oil in a wok and sauté spring onions, ginger, and garlic for 1 1/2 minutes. Remove. Add meat and fry on high heat until lightly coloured on both sides. Turn only once and do not overcook. Push to one side of pan and return onion, ginger, and garlic and add pre-mixed seasoning B/sauce.

Bring to boil, then simmer until thickened, stirring beef into sauce. Transfer to a warmed serving plate and garnish with fresh coriander. Serve at once.

SAUTÉED SHREDDED LAMB ON RICE NOODLES

185 g (6 oz) lean lamb *

5 cups (1¼ litres) deep-frying oil

45 g (1½ oz) rice vermicelli, broken

45 g (1½ oz) canned champignons, drained and sliced

30 g (1 oz) canned bamboo shoots, drained and shredded

1 medium green capsicum (bell pepper), trimmed and shredded

Seasoning A:

1 egg white, beaten

½ teaspoon salt

½ teaspoon bicarbonate of soda (optional)

1 tablespoon light soy sauce

2 teaspoons rice wine or dry sherry

1½ tablespoons finely chopped spring onion (scallion)

1 teaspoon grated fresh ginger

1 teaspoon cornflour (cornstarch)

Seasoning B/Sauce:

½ cup (4 fl oz) chicken stock

1 tablespoon light soy sauce

1 teaspoon rice wine or dry sherry

⅓ teaspoon sugar

pinch of white pepper

¼ teaspoon sugar

¾ teaspoon cornflour (cornstarch)

Partially freeze lamb and cut into thin slices, then into fine shreds. Place in a dish and add the seasoning A, mix well and leave to marinate for 20 minutes.

Heat oil to smoking point and fry broken rice vermicelli in a frying basket until it expands into a cloud of crisp white noodles, about 20 seconds. Drain well and place on a serving plate. Pour off all but 3 tablespoons of oil.

Reheat wok and sauté shredded lamb until it changes colour, push to one side of pan and sauté shredded vegetables for 2 minutes, then mix in lamb and add seasoning B/sauce, pre-mixed, and simmer until thickened. Pour over noodles and serve at once.

* Lean pork, beef fillet (tenderloin), or chicken breast can replace lamb in this dish.

Vegetables and Sweets

MIXED VEGETABLE PLATTER

	Seasoning/Sauce:
1 medium carrot	2/3 cup chicken stock
1 medium white onion	3/4 teaspoon salt
6 dried black mushrooms, soaked for 25 minutes	1/3 teaspoon chicken stock powder (optional)
6 canned water chestnuts, drained	3/4 teaspoon sugar
6 canned champignons, drained	1 1/4 teaspoons cornflour (cornstarch)
6 canned baby corn cobs, drained	
250 g (8 oz) fresh lettuce or Chinese (celery) cabbage	
1/3 cup frying oil	

Peel carrot, thinly slice lengthwise, then cut into rectangular pieces. Peel onion, cut in halves from stem to root, then cut into thick slices from stem to root and trim away root section to allow pieces to separate. Squeeze the water from mushrooms and remove stems. Slice water chestnuts and champignons in halves horizontally. Cut baby corn in halves. Thoroughly wash lettuce or cabbage, separating leaves.

Parboil carrot and drain well. Blanch onion for 20 seconds and drain well. Heat oil in a wok and stir-fry carrot and onions for 30 seconds. Push to one side of pan and add mushrooms, water chestnuts and champignons and stir-fry together for 1 minute, then add corn and mix vegetables together. Stir-fry on high heat for a further 30 seconds, then add pre-mixed seasoning/sauce and simmer until sauce thickens.

In the meantime, heat a saucepan of water to boiling and add 1 tablespoon of oil and a dash of salt. Add lettuce or cabbage and simmer until tender. Lettuce needs only about 45 seconds, cabbage a little longer. Drain well and arrange on a serving plate. Spoon vegetables on top and serve at once.

61

CHINESE CABBAGE WITH MINCED SHRIMP DRESSING

625 g (1¼ lb) fresh Chinese (celery) cabbage	**Seasoning B/Sauce:**
75 g (2½ oz) raw peeled shrimps	½ cup (4 fl oz) chicken stock
2 egg whites, beaten	1 teaspoon salt
¼ cup (2 fl oz) cold water	½ teaspoon m.s.g. (optional)
1 teaspoon cornflour (cornstarch)	¼ teaspoon white pepper
pinch of salt	½ teaspoon cornflour (cornstarch)
⅓ cup softened lard or frying oil	
Seasoning A:	
¼ cup (2 fl oz) chicken stock	
¾ teaspoon salt	
½ teaspoon m.s.g. (optional)	
¼ teaspoon sugar	
pinch of white pepper	

Wash cabbage well, discard outer leaves and cut lengthwise into quarters, or into smaller pieces if head is large. Blanch in boiling water for 1 minute, then drain well.

Chop shrimps in a food processor or by batting with side of a cleaver blade. Mix with egg whites, cold water, cornflour, and salt.

Sauté cabbage in half the lard for 2 minutes on moderate heat, then add seasoning A and simmer until liquid has evaporated. Remove from pan and arrange on a serving plate.

Add remaining lard to pan and sauté shrimp paste until it turns white, about 1 minute on moderate heat. Add pre-mixed seasoning B/sauce and bring to the boil. Simmer until thickened, then pour over cabbage and serve.

WONTONS IN SOUP WITH MIXED MEAT AND VEGETABLES

18 uncooked wontons	60 g (2 oz) cooked pork fillet or roast pork, shredded
4 cups (1 litre) chicken stock	
3 thick slices fresh ginger, shredded	6 stalks fresh young bok choy
1½ teaspoons salt	1 medium carrot, shredded
½ teaspoon m.s.g. (optional)	30 g (1 oz) canned bamboo shoots, drained and shredded
pinch of ground black pepper	
60 g (2 oz) cooked chicken breast, shredded	

Bring a large saucepan of salted water to the boil and add wontons. Simmer until they rise to the surface, then cook for 2½-3 minutes more. Drain and place in six soup bowls.

Bring stock to the boil and add ginger, salt, m.s.g., if used, and pepper. Simmer briefly, then add shredded meat and vegetables and simmer for 2½-3 minutes. Add sesame oil and divide soup among the bowls. Serve hot.

WATERCRESS AND LIVER SOUP

185 g (6 oz) fresh watercress	**Seasoning:**
125 g (4 oz) lamb or pork liver	1 spring onion (scallion), trimmed and shredded
4 cups (1 litre) chicken stock	2 slices fresh ginger, shredded
	¾ teaspoon salt
	¼ teaspoon m.s.g. (optional)
	1 tablespoon light soy sauce
	2 teaspoons rice wine or dry sherry

Remove stems from watercress. Cut liver into very thin slices and blanch in boiling water for 20 seconds, drain and soak in cold water for 5 minutes.

Bring chicken stock to the boil and add seasoning ingredients. Simmer for 2 minutes, then add sliced liver and simmer a further 2 minutes. Add watercress, stir in and cook until just softened. Pour into a soup tureen.

SAUTÉED CHINESE SPINACH WITH SHRIMP SAUCE

500 g (1 lb) fresh Chinese spinach*	2 teaspoons Chinese shrimp sauce**
1 spring onion (scallion), trimmed and shredded	¼ cup (2 fl oz) chicken stock
2 cloves garlic, chopped	½ teaspoon cornflour (cornstarch)
½ cup (2 fl oz) frying oil	

Thoroughly wash vegetables and cut into 7.5 cm (3 in) lengths. Heat oil and sauté spring onion and garlic briefly, then add spinach and sauté on moderate heat until tender. Stir in shrimp sauce (use more or less, to taste) and sautée briefly, then add chicken stock mixed with cornflour and simmer until sauce thickens.

Transfer to a serving plate and serve at once.

* A green leafy vegetable with narrow white stems similar to *bok choy*, which can be used as a substitute.

** A pale pink pungent sauce made by grinding and salting fresh shrimps, sun-drying, then storing in vats until fermented. If unobtainable, use anchovy sauce or essence.

LETTUCE WITH OYSTER SAUCE

1 large fresh lettuce	½ teaspoon salt
1½ tablespoons frying oil	2½ tablespoons oyster sauce*

Thoroughly wash lettuce and separate leaves. Bring a large saucepan of water to boil and add oil and salt. Add lettuce and simmer until tender, about 1½ minutes. Drain well and arrange on a serving plate.

Pour the oyster sauce evenly over lettuce and serve at once.

* Use a good quality oyster sauce, as the less expensive brands do not have the same rich flavour.

FRESH CELERY WITH CREAMY MUSTARD SAUCE

3 stalks fresh celery	**Sauce:**
½ teaspoon salt	½ cup (4 fl oz) chicken stock or water
	1 tablespoon evaporated milk
	2 tablespoons vegetable oil
	1-1½ teaspoons hot mustard powder
	½ teaspoon salt
	½ teaspoon sugar
	1¼ teaspoons cornflour (cornstarch)

String celery and cut into pieces about 4 cm (1⅔ in) long, then cut each piece lengthwise into two or three sticks. Blanch in boiling water with salt added, for 1 minute, then drain and refresh with cold water. Drain again and arrange on a serving plate.

Pour pre-mixed sauce into a wok and bring to the boil. Simmer until thickened, then pour over vegetables and serve at once.

SAUTÉED FRESH CHOY SUM

625 g (1¼ lb) fresh young choy sum*	⅓ teaspoon m.s.g. (optional)
2 tablespoons frying oil	½ teaspoon sugar
2 tablespoons rendered chicken fat (chicken grease) or lard	1½ teaspoons rice wine or dry sherry
¾ teaspoon salt	

Trim off any wilted leaves and cut *choy sum* into 5 cm (2 in) pieces. Peel thick skin from lower section of stems, if preferred. Simmer in boiling water for 2 minutes, then drain.

Heat oil and chicken fat in a wok and add salt, m.s.g., and sugar. Sauté vegetables on moderate heat for 2 minutes or until tender, then sizzle wine onto sides of pan, stir in and serve.

* Or use any fresh green vegetables.

65

STEWED WINTER MELON BALLS WITH SCALLOP SAUCE

6 dried scallops (about 45 g/1½ oz), soaked for 1 hour	**Seasoning/Sauce:**
½ cup (4 fl oz) chicken stock	1¼ cups (10 fl oz) chicken stock
1 thick slice fresh ginger	1 tablespoon rendered chicken fat (chicken grease) or lard
700 g (1⅓ lb) fresh winter melon*	2 teaspoons rice wine or dry sherry
cornflour (cornstarch)	1¼ teaspoons salt
	1½ teaspoons sugar
	¾ teaspoon m.s.g. (optional)

Place drained scallops in a dish and add chicken stock and ginger slice. Steam until tender, about 45 minutes, then remove scallops from stock and shred by rubbing between forefinger and thumb. Return to stock and set aside.

Peel melon and remove seeds. Cut into 2.5 cm (1 in) cubes or make into balls with a melon baller. Cover with boiling, slightly salted water and simmer for 20 minutes. Drain well.

Bring the seasoning/sauce to boil and add drained melon. Cover and simmer on low heat until the melon is completely tender, then transfer to a serving plate with a slotted spoon.

Bring sauce back to the boil, add drained scallops and simmer until reduced to about ¾ cup. Thicken with a thin paste of cornflour and cold water and simmer for 1 minute, then pour over melon and serve.

* Or use about 625 g (1¼ lb) canned winter melon or fresh sweet white turnips or cucumbers.

STEAMED WINTER MELON BALLS FILLED WITH VEGETABLES

1 1¼ kg) (2½ lb) winter melon, or use a large pumpkin	**Seasoning:**
60 g (2 oz) canned bamboo shoots, drained and cubed	2 cups (16 fl oz) chicken stock
	2 tablespoons oyster or light soy sauce
60 g (2 oz) canned straw mushrooms, drained and sliced	2 teaspoons rice wine or dry sherry
	1¼ teaspoons salt
60 g (2 oz) canned lotus roots, drained and cubed	½ teaspoon m.s.g. (optional)
1 medium carrot, parboiled and cubed	¾ teaspoon sugar
60 g (2 oz) canned champignons, drained and halved	
30 g (1 oz) canned gingko or white nuts, drained (optional)	
12 green vegetable hearts, trimmed and washed	
2 tablespoons chopped cooked ham	
1 tablespoon rendered chicken fat (chicken grease) or lard	

Wash winter melon, peel off skin very thinly so that the outside remains a bright green. Cut a section from top and scoop out seeds and pith. If using a pumpkin, do not peel until after it is cooked.

Fill with boiling lightly salted water and add 1 tablespoon of vegetable oil. Set in a dish and place on a rack. Cover and steam over rapidly boiling water for 20 minutes. Drain and fill with prepared vegetables, except green vegetables. Add seasoning ingredients and return to steamer.

Steam again over rapidly boiling water for 25 minutes or until melon is tender, but not softening too much to lose its shape. In the final 10 minutes of cooking, place green vegetables on top of other ingredients in melon.

To serve, place melon in centre of a serving dish and surround with green vegetables. Garnish with chopped ham and add chicken fat. Thicken sauce, if preferred, by straining into a wok, bring to the boil and adding a thin paste of cornflour and cold water.

STEAMED BROCCOLI
WITH CRABMEAT SAUCE

500 g (1 lb) fresh broccoli, trimmed
and cut into florets

¼ cup (2 fl oz) frying oil

60 g (2 oz) fresh crabmeat

1½ tablespoons chopped spring onion

⅓ teaspoon grated fresh ginger

2 teaspoons rice wine or dry sherry

2 egg whites, well beaten

chopped cooked ham (optional)

Seasoning A:

1 teaspoon salt

½ teaspoon m.s.g. (optional)

½ teaspoon sugar

1 teaspoon rice wine or dry sherry

¾ cup (6 fl oz) chicken stock

Seasoning B/Sauce:

¾ cup (6 fl oz) chicken stock

½ teaspoon salt

½ teaspoon m.s.g. (optional)

pinch of white pepper

½ teaspoon sugar

1 teaspoon cornflour (cornstarch)

Wash broccoli and drain well. Heat oil in a wok and sauté broccoli on moderate heat for 2 minutes, then remove and drain well. Transfer to a dish and add seasoning A and steam over rapidly boiling water for 10 minutes. Remove, drain and arrange on a serving plate.

Reheat wok and sauté crabmeat with spring onion and ginger for 1 minute. Sizzle wine onto sides of pan, then add pre-mixed seasoning B/sauce and bring to the boil.

Remove from heat and drizzle in beaten egg whites, allowing to set in sauce before stirring. Check seasonings and pour over broccoli. Garnish with chopped ham, if used, and serve.

BAMBOO SHOOTS WITH MUSHROOMS AND QUAIL EGGS

	Seasoning A:
6 dried black mushrooms, soaked for 25 minutes	**Seasoning A :**
125 g (4 oz) canned bamboo shoots, drained and thinly sliced	⅓ teaspoon salt
	½ teaspoon m. s. g. (optional)
½ cup (4 fl oz) chicken stock	⅓ teaspoon sugar
60 g (2 oz) canned straw mushrooms, drained and sliced	¼ cup (2 fl oz) chicken stock
	Seasoning B/Sauce :
90 g (3 oz) canned quail eggs, drained	⅔ cup chicken stock
2 tablespoons frying oil	2 teaspoons light soy sauce
1 spring onion (scallion), trimmed and shredded	1 teaspoon rice wine or dry sherry
2 slices fresh ginger, shredded	1 teaspoon sesame oil (optional)
	½ teaspoon sugar
	2 teaspoons cornflour (cornstarch)

Squeeze water from mushrooms, remove stems and cut caps into quarters. Mix with seasoning A and steam for 20 minutes. Drain.

Blanch bamboo shoots in boiling water. Drain well and soak in chicken stock with sliced straw mushrooms and quail eggs.

Heat oil in wok and fry spring onion and ginger for 1 minute, then add pre-mixed seasoning B/sauce and bring to the boil. Add drained vegetables and eggs and simmer until sauce thickens.

PLAIN WHITE RICE

The absorption method of cooking rice is the one most often used by Chinese.

A fairly heavy-based saucepan with a very tight-fitting lid is used. The rice is placed in dry, water added and the lid placed securely. When water comes to the boil, heat is turned to low and rice left to cook until water is completely absorbed, leaving rice dry, fluffy, and each grain separate, but sticky enough to cling together for easy eating with chopsticks.

Allow 90 g (3 oz/½ cup) short grain rice per person and place in a saucepan. Add salt, though most Chinese prefer their rice unsalted, and water to cover rice by 2 cm (¾ in). The rice should be smoothed flat to accurately gauge water level. For more accurate measurement, use 2 cups rice and 3 cups water. (Two cups of raw short grain rice make 5 cups cooked rice.)

SWEET RICE BALLS IN RED BEAN SOUP

1 cup glutinous rice powder	1 280 g (9 oz) can sweet red bean paste
¼ cup (2 fl oz) boiling water	1 cup sugar (or to taste)
1 tablespoon sugar	4 cups (1 litre) water
1 tablespoon softened lard	
1½-2 tablespoons cold water	

Place rice powder in a mixing bowl and add boiling water, sugar, and lard. Work with handle of a wooden spoon until well mixed, then add cold water to make a smooth, fairly hard dough. Knead for 2 minutes, then roll out into a long sausage shape and cut into small pieces. Roll each piece into a ball.

Bring a large saucepan of water to the boil and add rice balls. Simmer until they rise to the surface, about 3 minutes, then remove with a slotted spoon into a dish of cold water.

Mix red bean paste with sugar and water. Heat to boiling and reduce to a simmer. Add rice balls and simmer for about 3 minutes, then serve hot.

GLAZED SWEET POTATO BALLS WITH SESAME SEEDS

500 g (1 lb) sweet potato or yams	5 cups (1¼ litres) deep-frying oil
2 whole eggs, beaten	½ cup toasted white sesame seeds
½ cup cornflour (cornstarch)	1½ cups sugar

Peel sweet potato and form into small balls using a melon scoop. Soak in cold water for 20 minutes, then dry thoroughly and coat very lightly with cornflour. Dip into beaten egg and coat again with cornflour. Heat oil to moderately hot and deep-fry potato balls for 3 minutes. Remove and drain well.

Transfer about 2 tablespoons of oil to another wok and add sugar. Stir on moderate heat until sugar melts and turns into a thick golden syrup. Remove from heat.

Reheat oil and fry potato balls for a second time until cooked through, about 2 minutes, then transfer to syrup. Carefully turns balls in syrup until evenly coated.

Spread sesame seeds on a piece of greaseproof paper. Add the glazed sweet potato balls and turn until thickly coated. Transfer to an oiled serving plate and serve while still hot.

EGG CUSTARD

6 whole eggs	1½ tablespoons clear honey or white sugar
3 egg whites	2 teaspoons cornflour (cornstarch)
1½ cups (12 fl oz) fresh milk	¾ teaspoon grated lemon rind

Beat eggs and egg whites well together, then add milk, honey, and cornflour and beat to a smooth batter. Stir in lemon rind, then pour mixture into a greased ovenproof dish or six individual heatproof dessert dishes. Set on a rack and steam over gently boiling water for about 15 minutes, or until just set. Serve immediately.

ALMOND JELLY WITH FRESH FRUIT

⅔ cup boiling water	2 teaspoons almond essence
1⅓ tablespoons unflavoured gelatine	250 g (8 oz) diced fresh fruit, chilled
1½ cups (12 fl oz) lukewarm water or milk	⅓ cup liquid from canned fruit or sugar syrup
⅓ cup evaporated milk or fresh cream	

Mix boiling water and gelatine together and stir slowly until dissolved, then add water, evaporated milk and almond essence and mix thoroughly.

Pour into a lightly oiled jelly mould and leave to set. Chill thoroughly.

Turn jelly out onto a serving plate and surround with diced fruit. Pour on fruit or sugar syrup and serve.

ALMOND AND QUAIL EGG TEA

12 canned or fresh quail eggs	1 tablespoon Chinese black tea leaves
60 g (2 oz) blanched almonds	1 cup sugar
1 teaspoon bicarbonate of soda	1 10 cm (4 in) cinnamon stick

Boil fresh quail eggs, if used, in water for about 4½ minutes until firm. Cool under running cold water and remove shells. Drain canned eggs. Cover with cold water and set aside.

Place almonds and bicarbonate of soda in a saucepan and add about 1½ cups of water. Bring to the boil and simmer until almonds are tender, about 45 minutes. Drain well and rinse with clean cold water.

Brew half the tea with 1 cup boiling water. Place remaining tea in a bowl and add one-quarter of the sugar and the drained eggs. Add boiling water to cover and place in a steamer.

Place cinnamon stick in another bowl and set in steamer also. Cover and steam over rapidly boiling water for 25 minutes.

Bring 2 cups of water to the boil and add remaining sugar, stirring until dissolved.

Into 6 dessert bowls divide almonds and place 2 drained eggs in each. Add a splash each of tea and cinnamon water and top up with sugar water. Serve hot.

This is an unusual blend of ingredients for a sweet dish, but the result is a cooling, refreshing dessert which can also be served chilled.

If preferred, substitute poached fruit or softened lotus seeds for the quail eggs.

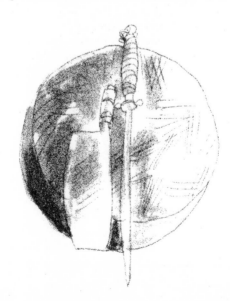